Pocket
Dictionary

Pitman New Era Shorthand

PITMAN PUBLISHING LIMITED
128 Long Acre, London WC2E 9AN

Associated Companies
Pitman Publishing Pty Ltd, Melbourne
Pitman Publishing New Zealand Ltd, Wellington

Text set in 6 pt Monotype Old Style, printed and
bound in Great Britain at The Pitman Press, Bath

ISBN 0 273 40954 9

INTRODUCTORY NOTE

The present work is an abridgment of PITMAN SHORTHAND DICTIONARY, by SIR ISAAC PITMAN. It is designed to provide, in a size suitable for pocket use, a guide to the best shorthand outlines for approximately 20,000 of the more common words in the English language. The outlines are given in vocalized shorthand, except for short forms and any portions of derivative or compound words for which short forms are retained.

In addition, about 1,000 of the most useful words have been selected from the Appendix to PITMAN ENGLISH AND SHORTHAND DICTIONARY and entered in their appropriate alphabetical places.

A

aback'
aban'don
aban'doned
aban'doning
aban'donment
abash'
abashed'
abate'
aba'ted
abate'ment
abat'ing
abattoir'
ab'bot
abbre'viate
abbre'viated
abbre'viating
abbrevia'tion
ab'dicate
ab'dicated
ab'dicating
abdica'tion
abdo'men
abdom'inal
abduct'
abduct'ed
abduct'ing
abduc'tion
aberra'tion
abey'ance
abhor'
abhorred'
abhor'rence
abhor'rent
abhor'ring
abide'
abid'ing
abil'ity
ab'ject
ab'jectly

ablaze'
a'ble
a'ble-bodied
ablu'tion
a'bly
abnor'mal
abnormal'ity
aboard'
abode'
abol'ish
abol'ished
abol'ishing
abol'ishment
aboli'tion
abom'inable
abom'inate
abom'inated
abomina'tion
aborig'inal
abor'tive
abound'
abound'ed
abound'ing
about'
above'
abra'sion
abreast'
abridge'
abridged'
abridg'ing
abridg'ment
abroad'
ab'rogate
abroga'tion
abrupt'
abrupt'ly
abrupt'ness
ab'scess
abscond'
abscond'ed

5

abscond'er
abscond'ing
ab'sence
ab'sent, *a.*
absent', *v.*
absent'ed
absentee'
ab'solute
ab'solutely
absolu'tion
absolve'
absorb'
absorbed'
absorb'ent
absorb'ing
absorp'tion
abstain'
abstain'er
abstain'ing
abste'mious
absten'tion
ab'stinence
abstract', *v.*
ab'stract, *a. & n.*
abstract'ed
abstract'ing
abstrac'tion
abstruse'
absurd'
absurd'ity
absurd'ly
abun'dance
abun'dant
abun'dantly
abuse'
abused'
abus'ing
abu'sive
abu'sively
abut'
abyss'
academ'ic
academ'ical
acad'emy
accede'
acced'ed
acced'ing

accel'erate
accel'erated
accel'erating
accelera'tion
accel'erator
ac'cent, *n.*
accent', *v.*
accent'ed
accent'ing
accent'uate
accent'uated
accentua'tion
accept'
accept'able
accept'ance
accept'ed
accept'ing
ac'cess
accessibil'ity
acces'sible
acces'sion
ac'cessory
ac'cident
acciden'tal
acclaim'
acclama'tion
accli'matize
accli'matized
accli'matizing
accom'modate
accom'modated
accom'modat-
    ing
accommoda'-
    tion
accom'panied
accom'pani-
    ment
accom'panist
accom'pany
accom'panying
accom'plice
accom'plish
accom'plished
accom'plishing
accom'plish-
    ment
accord'

accord'ance	
accord'ed	
accord'ing	
accord'ingly	
accord'ion	
account'	
account'able	
account'ancy	
account'ant	
account'ed	
account'ing	
accred'ited	
accre'tion	
accrue'	
accrued'	
accru'ing	
accu'mulate	
accu'mulated	
accu'mulating	
accumula'tion	
accu'mulator	
ac'curacy	
ac'curate	
ac'curately	
accusa'tion	
accuse'	
accused'	
accus'ing	
accus'tom	
accus'tomed	
ace	
acerb'ity	
acet'ylene	
ache	
ached	
achieve'	
achieved'	
achieve'ment	
achiev'ing	
ach'ing	
ac'id	
acid'ity	
acidos'is	
acknowl'edge	
acknowl'edged	
acknowl'edging	
acknowl'edg-	
ment	

ac'me	
a'corn	
acous'tic	
acquaint'	
acquaint'ance	
acquaint'ed	
acquaint'ing	
acquiesce'	
acquies'cence	
acquire'	
acquired'	
acquire'ment	
acquir'ing	
acquisi'tion	
acquis'itive	
acquit'	
acquit'tal	
acquit'ted	
acquit'ting	
a'cre	
a'creage	
ac'rid	
acrimo'nious	
ac'robat	
acrobat'ic	
ac'ronym	
across'	
act	
act'ed	
act'ing	
actin'ium	
ac'tion	
ac'tionable	
ac'tivate	
ac'tive	
ac'tively	
activ'ity	
act'or	
act'ress	
act'ual	
act'ually	
ac'tuary	
acu'ity	
acu'men	
acute'	
acute'ly	
ad'age	
ad'amant	

adapt'	
adaptabil'ity	
adapt'able	
adapta'tion	
adapt'ed	
adapt'ing	
add	
ad'ded	
addict'	
addic'ted	
ad'ding	
addi'tion	
addi'tional	
address'	
addressed'	
addressee'	
address'ing	
adept'	
ad'equacy	
ad'equate	
ad'equately	
adhere'	
adhered'	
adhe'rence	
adhe'rent	
adhe'ring	
adhe'sion	
adhe'sive	
adhe'siveness	
adieu'	
adja'cent	
adja'cently	
ad'jective	
adjoin'	
adjoin'ing	
adjourn'	
adjourned'	
adjourn'ing	
adjourn'ment	
adju'dicate	
adjudica'tion	
ad'junct	
adjust'	
adjust'ed	
adjust'ing	
adjust'ment	
admin'ister	
admin'istered	

admin'istering	
admin'istrate	
administra'tion	
admin'istra-tive	
admin'istrator	
ad'mirable	
ad'miral	
ad'miralty	
admira'tion	
admire'	
admired'	
admir'er	
admir'ing	
admir'ingly	
admis'sible	
admis'sion	
admit'	
admit'tance	
admit'ted	
admit'ting	
admon'ish	
admon'ished	
admon'ishing	
admoni'tion	
adoles'cence	
adoles'cent	
adopt'	
adopt'ed	
adopt'ing	
adop'tion	
ador'able	
adora'tion	
adore'	
ador'ing	
adorn'	
adorned'	
adorn'ing	
adorn'ment	
adre'nal	
adren'alin	
adult'	
adul'terate	
adul'terated	
adultera'tion	
adult'hood	
advance'	

advanced'	affect'
advance'ment	affecta'tion
advan'cing	affect'ed
advan'tage	affec'tion
advanta'geous	affec'tionate
advanta'ge-ously	affec'tionately
adventi'tious	affida'vit
adven'ture	affil'iate
adven'turer	affil'iated
adven'turess	affilia'tion
ad'verb	affirm'
ad'versary	affirm'ative
ad'verse	affirmed'
ad'versely	affirm'ing
adver'sity	affix', v.
ad'vertise	af'fix, n.
ad'vertised	affixed'
adver'tise-ment	affix'ing
ad'vertiser	afflict'
ad'vertising	afflict'ed
advice'	afflict'ing
advisabil'ity	afflic'tion
advis'able	af'fluently
advise'	afford'
advised'	afford'ed
advis'edly	afford'ing
advis'er	afforesta'tion
advis'ing	affront'
advis'ory	affront'ed
ad'vocacy	afloat'
ad'vocate, n.	afore'said
ad'vocate, v.	afraid'
ad'vocated	afresh'
ae'rial	Af'rican
aerobat'ics	Afrikaans'
aer'obus	**Afrikan'der**
aer'odrome	aft'er
aer'ofoil	aft'ermath
aeronau'tic	afternoon'
aer'oplane	aft'erwards
aesthet'ic	again'
aesthet'ics	against'
affabil'ity	age
af'fable	a'ged
af'fably	a'gency
affair'	agen'da
	a'gent

aggrand'ize-
ment
ag'gravate
ag'gravated
ag'gravating
aggrava'tion
ag'gregate
ag'gregated
ag'gregating
aggrega'tion
aggres'sion
aggress'ive
aggress'or
aggrieve'
aggrieved'
aghast'
ag'ile
agil'ity
ag'itate
ag'itated
ag'itating
agita'tion
ag'itator
agita'to
agnos'tic
ago'
ag'onizing
ag'ony
agree'
agree'able
agreed'
agree'ing
agree'ment
agricul'tural
ag'riculture
agricul'turist
aground'
a'gue
ah
ahead'
aid
aid'ed
aide-mém'oire
aid'ing
ail
ailed
ail'ing

ail'ment
aim
aimed
aim'ing
aim'less
aim'lessly
aim'lessness
air
air'borne
air'craft
air'field
air'force
air'-hole
air'-lift
air'line
air'mail
air'minded
air'plane
air'port
air-shaft
air'ship
air'strip
air'tight
air'way
air'worthi'ness
air'worthy
aisle
akin'
à la carte'
alac'rity
alarm'
alarmed'
alarm'ing
alarm'ingly
alas'
al'bum
al'cohol
alcohol'ic
al'derman
ale
alert'
alert'ness
al'gebra
a'lias
al'ibi
a'lien
a'lienate
a'lienated

a'lienating		allud'ed	
aliena'tion		allud'ing	
alight'		allure'	
alight'ed		allur'ing	
alight'ing		allur'ingly	
align', aline'		allu'sion	
align'ment		allu'via	
alike'		al'ly	
aliment'ary		al'manac	
al'imony		*al*might'y	
alive'		a'lmond	
al'kali		*al'most*	
al'kaline		aloft'	
all		alone'	
allay'		along'	
allayed'		along'side	
allay'ing		aloof'	
allega'tion		aloud'	
allege'		al'phabet	
alleged'		alphabet'ic	
alle'giance		alphabet'ical	
alleg'ing		Alp'ine	
all'ergy		*al*read'y	
alle'viate		al'so	
alle'viated		al'tar	
alle'viating		al'ter	
allevia'tion		altera'tion	
al'ley		alterca'tion	
al'leyway		al'tered	
alli'ance		al'tering	
al'lied		al'ternate, *v.*	
al'lies		altern'ate, *a.*	
al'locate		al'ternated	
al'located		altern'ately	
al'locating		al'ternating	
alloca'tion		altern'ative	
allot'		altern'atively	
allot'ment		al'ternator	
allot'ropism		*although'*	
allot'ted		al'titude	
allot'ting		*altogeth'er*	
allow'		al'truism	
allow'able		altruis'tic	
allow'ance		alumin'ium	
allowed'		alu'minum	
allow'ing		*al'*ways	
alloy'		am	
allude'		*amal'gamate*	

amal'gamated	among'
amal'gamating	amongst'
amalgama'tion	amo'ral
amanuen'sis	amoral'ity
amass'	amortiza'tion
amassed'	amor'tize
amass'ing	amor'tizement
am'ateur	amount'
amaze'	amount'ed
amazed'	amount'ing
amaze'ment	amp'
amaz'ing	amper'age
amaz'ingly	amphib'ian
Am'azon	amphithe'atre
ambas'sador	am'ple
am'ber	amplifica'tion
ambigu'ity	am'plified
ambig'uous	am'plifier
ambig'uously	am'plify
ambi'tion	am'plifying
ambi'tious	am'ply
ambi'tiously	am'poule
ambiv'alence	am'putate
ambiv'alent	am'putated
am'bulance	am'putating
am'bush	amputa'tion
ame'liorate	amuse'
ameliora'tion	amused'
amen'	amuse'ment
ame'nable	amus'ing
ame'nably	*an*
amend'	anach'ronism
amend'ed	anae'mia
amend'ment	anaem'ic
amen'ity	anaesthet'ic
Amer'ican	analges'ic
Amer'icanism	anal'ogous
a'miable	anal'ogy
am'icable	an'alyse
am'icably	an'alysed
amid'	an'alysing
amidst'	anal'ysis
amiss'	an'alyst
am'ity	analyt'ic
ammo'nia	analyt'ical
ammuni'tion	an'archist
amoe'bic	an'archy
amok'	anath'ema

anatom'ical
anat'omy
an'cestor
ances'tral
anch'or
anch'ored
anch'oring
an'cient
and
an'ecdote
ane'mic
 anae'mic
anesthet'ic
 anaesthet'ic
anew'
an'gel
angel'ic
an'ger
an'gered
an'gle
Ang'lophil
Ang'lophile
Ang'lophobe
ango'ra
an'grily
an'gry
an'guish
an'gular
angular'ity
an'iline
an'imal
an'imate
an'imated
an'imating
anima'tion
animos'ity
an'iseed
an'kle
an'nals
annex'
annexa'tion
annexed'
annex'ing
anni'hilate
anni'hilated
anni'hilating
annihila'tion
anniver'sary

an'notate
an'notated
an'notating
annota'tion
announce'
announced'
announce'-
 ment
announc'er
announc'ing
annoy'
annoy'ance
annoyed'
annoy'ing
an'nual
an'nually
annu'ity
annul'
annul'ling
an'num
anom'alous
anom'aly
anonym'ity
anon'ymous
anon'ymously
anoph'eles
anoth'er
an'swer
an'swerable
an'swered
an'swering
antag'onism *or*
antag'onist *or*
antagonist'ic *or*
antag'onize
Antarc'tic *or*
antece'dent
an'tedate
an'tedated
antenat'al
an'them
anthol'ogist
anthol'ogy
an'thracite
an'thrax

anti-air'craft	
antibiot'ic	
an'tic	
antic'ipate	
antic'ipated	
antic'ipating	
anticipa'tion	
an'tidote	
antihist'amine	
an'tiquated	
antique'	
antiq'uity	
anti-semit'ic	
antisep'tic	
antith'esis	
anti-vivisec'tion	
ant'ler	
an'vil	
anxi'ety	
anx'ious	
anx'iously	
an'y	
an'ybody	
an'yhow	
an'yone	
an'ytime	
an'ything	
an'yway	
an'ywhere	
apart'	
apart'heid	
apart'ment	
apathet'ic	
ap'athy	
ape'ritif	
ap'erture	
a'pex	
aph'orism	
aphrodis'iac	
apiece'	
apologet'ic	
apolo'gia	
apol'ogize	
apol'ogized	
apol'ogizing	
apol'ogy	
apos'tle	
appal'	

appalled'	
appall'ing	
appara'tus	
appar'el	
appar'ent	
appa'rently	
appeal'	
appealed'	
appeal'ing	
appear'	
appear'ance	
appeared'	
appear'ing	
appease'	
appel'lant	
appel'late	
appella'tion	
append'	
append'age	
append'ed	
appen'dices	
appendici'tis	
append'ing	
appen'dix	
appen'dixes	
appertain'	
appertained'	
appertain'ing	
ap'petite	
ap'petize	
ap'petizing	
applaud'	
applaud'ed	
applaud'ing	
applause'	
ap'ple	
appli'ance	
ap'plicable or	
ap'plicant	
applica'tion	
applied'	
apply'	
apply'ing	
appoint'	
appoint'ed	
appoint'ing	
appoint'ment	

appor'tion
appor'tioned
appor'tioning
appor'tion-
  ment
ap'posite
apprais'al
appraise'
appraised'
appre'ciable
appre'ciate
appre'ciated
appre'ciating
apprecia'tion
appre'ciative
apprehend'
apprehend'ed
apprehend'ing
apprehen'sion
apprehen'sive
appren'tice
appren'ticed
appren'tice-
  ship
approach'
approach'able
approached'
approach'ing
approba'tion
appro'priate
appro'priated
appro'priately
appro'priate-
  ness
appro'priating
appropria'tion
approv'al
approve'
approved'
approv'ing
approv'ingly
approx'imate
approx'imated
approx'imately
approx'imat-
  ing
approxima'-
  tion

A'pril
a'pron
apropos'
apt
apt'itude
apt'ly
apt'ness
a'qualung
aquamarine'
a'qua-planing
aqua'rium
aquat'ic
a'queduct
Ar'ab
Ara'bian
Ar'abic
ar'able
ar'biter
arb'itrage
ar'bitrarily
ar'bitrary
ar'bitrate
ar'bitrated
ar'bitrating
arbitra'tion
ar'bitrator
arbor'eal
ar'bour, ar'bor
arc
arcade'
arch
archa'ic
archbish'op

{ *ar'chitect*
  architect'ural
  ar'chitecture

arc'-lamp
Arc'tic
ar'dent
ar'dently
ar'dour, ar'dor
ar'duous
are
a'rea
are'na
Ar'gentine
ar'gosy

ar'gue	arrest'ed
ar'gued	arrest'ing
ar'guing	arri'val
ar'gument	arrive'
argumen'ta-	arrived'
tive	arriv'ing
ar'id	ar'rogance
arid'ity	ar'rogant
aright'	ar'rogantly
arise'	ar'row
aris'en	ar'senal
aris'ing	ar'senic
aristoc'racy	ar'son
ar'istocrat	art
aristocrat'ic	ar'tery
arith'metic	arte'sian
arithmet'ical	art'ful
arm	ar'ticle
Armagedd'on	art'ifact
ar'mament	art'ifice
ar'mature	artifi'cial
arm'chair	artil'lery
armed	ar'tisan
arm'ing	art'ist
arm'istice	artist'ic
ar'mour,	ar'tistry
ar'mor	art'less
arms	as
ar'my	asbes'tos
aro'ma	ascend'
arose'	ascen'dancy
around'	ascend'ency
arouse'	ascertain'
aroused'	ascertained'
arous'ing	ascet'ic
arraign'	ascor'bic
arraigned'	ascribe'
arrange'	ascribed'
arranged'	ascrib'ing
arrange'ment	ash
arrang'ing	ashamed'
array'	ashore'
arrayed'	A'sian
arrear'	Asiat'ic
arrears'	aside'
arrest'	asinin'ity
	ask
	askance'

asked		assign'	
asleep'		assigned'	
as'pect		assignee'	
asper'sion		*assign'ment*	
as'phalt		assignor'	
asphyxia'tion		assigns'	
aspi'rant		assim'ilate	
as'pirate, *n.*		assim'ilated	
as'pirate, *v.*		assim'ilating	
aspira'tion		assimila'tion	
aspire'		assist'	
aspired'		assist'ance	
aspir'in		assist'ant	
aspir'ing		assist'ed	
assail'		assist'ing	
assail'ant		assize'	
assailed'		assiz'es	
assail'ing		asso'ciate	
assas'sin		asso'ciated	
assas'sinate		asso'ciating	
assas'sinated		associa'tion	
assault'		assort'	
assault'ed		assort'ed	
assault'ing		assort'ing	
assay'		assort'ment	
assayed'		assuage'	
assay'er		assume'	
assay'ing		assumed'	
assem'ble		assum'ing	
assem'bled		assump'tion	
assem'bling		assur'ance	
assem'bly		assure'	
assent'		assured'	
assent'ed		assur'edly	
assent'ing		assur'ing	
assert'		as'ter	
assert'ed		as'terisk	
assert'ing		asth'ma	
asser'tion		astir'	
assess'		aston'ish	or
assessed'		aston'ished	or
assess'ing		aston'ishing	or
assess'ment		aston'ishment	or
assess'or		astound'	
as'sets		astound'ed	
assidu'ity		astrakhan	
assid'uous			
assid'uously			

astray'	
astrin'gent	
as'trodome	
astrol'ogy	
as'tronaut	
astronaut'ics	
astron'omer	
astron'omy	
astute'	
asun'der	
asy'lum	
at	
ate	
a'theist	
ath'lete	
athlet'ic	
athlet'ics	
Atlan'tic	
At'las, at'las	
at'mosphere	
atmospher'ic	
atmosphe'rics	
at'om	
at'omizer	
aton'al	
atone'	
atoned'	
atone'ment	
atro'cious	
atro'ciously	
atroc'ity	
at'rophy	
attach'	
attached'	
attach'ing	
attach'ment	
attack'	
attacked'	
attack'ing	
attain'	
attain'able	
attained'	
attain'ing	
attain'ment	
attempt'	
attempt'ed	
attempt'ing	
attend'	

attend'ance	
attend'ant	
attend'ed	
attend'ing	
atten'tion	
atten'tive	
atten'tively	
atten'uate	
attest'	
attesta'tion	
attest'ed	
attest'er,	
attest'or	
attest'ing	
at'tic	
attire'	
attired'	
at'titude	
attor'ney	
Attor'ney- *Gen'eral*	
attract'	
attract'ed	
attract'ing	
attrac'tion	
attract'ive	
attract'ively	
attrib'utable	
ʃat'tribute, *n.*	
⎨attrib'ute, *v.*	
attrib'uted	
attrib'uting	
au'burn	
auc'tion	
auc'tioneer'	
auda'cious	
auda'ciously	
audac'ity	
audibil'ity	
au'dible	
au'dience	
au'dio	
au'dit	
au'dited	
au'diting	
au'ditor	
audito'rium	
aught	

augment′	automot′ive
augment′ed	auto-sugges′tion
augment′ing	au′tumn
au′gur	autum′nal
au′gured	auxil′iary
{Au′gust, n.	avail′
{august′, adj.	avail′able
aunt	availed′
au′ral	avail′ing
au′spices	av′alanche
auspi′cious	av′arice
	avari′cious
auspi′ciously	avenge′
	avenged′
Australa′sian	av′enue
Austra′lian	aver′
Aus′trian	av′erage
aut′archy	av′eraged
authen′tic	av′eraging
authen′ticate	averse′
authen′ticated	aver′sion
authentic′ity	avert′
au′thor	avert′ed
au′thoress	avert′ing
authoritar′ian	avia′tion
authori-	a′viator
tar′ianism	a′viatrix
author′itative	av′id
author′ita-	av′idly
tively	avoca′do
author′ity	avoca′tion
authoriza′tion	avoid′
au′thorize	avoid′able
au′thorized	avoid′ance
au′thorizing	avoid′ed
au′thorship	avoid′ing
aut′o	avoirdupois′
autobiograph′-	avow′
ical	avow′al
autobiog′raphy	await′
autoc′racy	await′ed
au′tocrat	await′ing
autocrat′ic	awake′
au′tograph	awa′ken
aut′omate	awa′kened
automat′ic	awa′kening
automa′tion	award′
autom′aton	award′ed
automobile′	

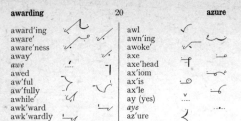

award'ing	awl
aware'	awn'ing
aware'ness	awoke'
away'	axe
awe	axe'head
awed	ax'iom
aw'ful	ax'is
aw'fully	ax'le
awhile'	ay (yes)
awk'ward	*aye*
awk'wardly	az'ure

B

bab'ble	
ba'by	
bab'y-sitt'er	
bach'elor	
bacil'lus	
back	
back'ben'cher	
back'bone	
back'chat	
back'cloth	
back'fire	
back'ground	
back'log	
back'marker	
back'*num'ber*	
back'scratch'er	
back'wards	
ba'con	
bacte'ria	
bacteriol'ogist	
bad	
bade	
badge	
bad'ly	
baf'fle	
baf'fled	
baf'fling	
bag	
bag'gage	
bag'pipe	
bail	
bailed	
bai'liff	
bait	
bait'ing	
bake	
bak'er	
bak'ery	
bak'ing	
bal'ance	

bal'anced	
bal'ance-sheet	
bal'ancing	
bal'cony	
bald	
bald'headed	
bald'ly	
bale	
baled	
balk	
ball	
bal'lad	
bal'last	
ballerin'a	
balletomane'	
balletoma'nia	
balloon'	
bal'lot	
bal'loted	
ballyhoo'	
balm'y	
bal'sa	
bamboo'	
ban	
bana'na	
band	
band'age	
band'aging	
band'ed	
band'master	
band'saw	
band'wag'on	
bang	
banged	
ban'ish	
ban'ished	
ban'ishment	
bank	
bank'book	
banked	

bank'er	bar'ter
bank'ing	bar'tered
bank'rupt	bar'tering
bank'ruptcy	bas'cule
ban'ner	base
ban'quet	base'ball
ban'ter	based
bap'tism	base'less
	base'ment
Bap'tist	bash'ful
	ba'sic
baptize'	bas'ically
	ba'sin
baptized'	ba'sing
	ba'sis
bar	bas'ket
barathe'a	bas'ketball
barbar'ic	bat
bar'barous	batch
bar'ber	bath
barb'itone	bathe
barbiturate'	bath'er
bare	bath'ing
bared	bath'room
bare'faced	bath'yscaphe
bare'ly	bath'ysphere
bar'est	bat'tery
bar'gain	bat'tle
bar'gaining	bat'tleship
barge	baulk
bar'ing	baux'ite
bark	Bava'rian
bark'ing	bay
bar'ley	bazaar
barn	*be*
barom'eter	beach
baromet'ric	beach'-comber
baroque'	bea'con
bar'rage	bead
barred	beak
bar'rel	beam
bar'ren	beamed
barricade'	bean
barrica'ded	bean'o
barrica'ding	bear
bar'rier	bear'able
bar'ring	beard
bar'row	beard'ed

bear'er	befriend'ed
bear'ing	befriend'ing
beast	beg
beast'ly	began'
beat	beg'gar
beat'en	beg'ging
beat'ing	begin'
beau'tified	begin'ner
beau'tiful	begin'ning
beau'tify	begrudge'
beau'tifying	begrudg'ing
beau'ty	beguile'
bea'ver	beguiled'
became'	begun'
because'	*behalf'*
beck'on	*behave'*
beck'oned	beha'ving
beck'oning	behav'iour,
become'	behav'ior
*be*com'ing	behav'iourism
bed	behav'iourist
bed'ding	beheld'
bed'pan	behind'
bedrag'gle	behold'
bedrag'gled	behoove'
bed'rock	beige
bed'room	*be'ing*
bed'sit'ter	belat'ed
bed'spread	bel'fry
bed'stead	Bel'gian
bed'time	*belief'*
bee	*believ'*able
beech	{*believe'*
beef	{*believed'*
bee'hive	believ'er
been	*believ'*ing
beer	belit'tle
beet	belit'tled
beet'le	bell
befall'	bellig'erent
befal'len	bel'low
befell'	bel'lowing
befit	bell'push
befit'ted	belong'
befit'ting	belonged'
before	belong'ing
before'*hand* *or*	beloved'
befriend'	belov'ed

below'	best	
belt	bestow'	
bench	bestowed'	
bend	bet	
bend'able	bête-noire	
bend'ing	betray'	
beneath'	betray'al	
benedic'tion	betroth'	
benefac'tor	betroth'al	
benefac'tress	betrothed'	
benef'icence	bet'ter	
benef'icent	bet'tering	
benef'icently	bet'terment	
benefi'cial	bet'ting	
benefi'ciary	between'	
ben'efit	betwixt'	
ben'efited	bev'el	
ben'efiting	bev'elled,	
benev'olence	bev'eled	
	bev'erage	
benev'olent	beware'	
	bewil'der	
benign'	bewil'dered	
benig'nant	bewil'dering	
	bewil'derment	
benign'ly	*beyond'*	
bent	bian'nual	
ben'zine	bi'as	
bequeath'	bi'ased	
bequeathed'	Bi'ble	
bequeath'ing	Bib'lical	
bequest'	bibliog'raphy	
bereave'	bi'cycle	
bereaved'	bid	
bereave'ment	bid'der	
bereft'	bid'ding	
ber'et	bien'nial	
ber'ry	bifo'cal	
ber'serk	bifo'cals	
berth	big	
beseech'	big'amist	
beseech'ing	big'amous	
beset'	big'amy	
beset'ting	big'ger	
beside'	big'gest	
besides'	big'ot	
besiege'	big'oted	
besieg'ing	big'otry	

bikin'i	
biling'ualism	
bil'ious	
bil'iousness	
bill	
billed	
bil'let	
bill'iards	
bil'lion	
bil'low	
bimet'allism,	
bimet'alism	
bind	
bind'er	
bind'ery	
bind'ing	
bing'o	
binoc'ular	
biochem'ical	
biochem'ist	
biochem'istry	
biog'rapher	
biograph'ic	
biograph'ical	
biog'raphy	
biolog'ical	
biol'ogy	
bi'plane	
birch	
bird	
bird's'-eye	
birth	
birth'-control	
birth'day	
birth'mark	
birth'place	
birth'rate	
birth'right	
bis'cuit	
bisect'	
bisect'ed	
bisect'ing	
bish'op	
bis'muth	
bit	
bite	
bit'ing	

bit'ten	
bit'ter	
bit'terness	
bitu'minous	
bizarre'	
black	
black'berry	
black'bird	
black'board	
black'en	
black'ened	
black'ening	
black'guard	
black'mail	
black'smith	
blad'der	
blade	
blame	
blamed	
blame'less	
blame'worthy	
blank	
blank'et	
blaspheme'	
blasphemed'	
blas'phemous	
blas'phemy	
blast	
blast'ed	
blast'ing	
bla'tant	
blaze	
blazed	
blaz'er	
bleach	
bleach'ing	
bleak	
bled	
bleed	
bleed'ing	
blem'ish	
blend	
blend'ed	
bless	
blessed	
bless'ed	
bless'ing	
blest	

blew	blun'der
blight	blun'dered
blight'ed	blun'dering
blight'ing	blunt
blind	blunt'ed
blind'ed	blunt'ly
blind'fold	blur
blind'folded	blurred
blind'ing	blur'ring
blind'ly	blurt
blind'ness	blurt'ed
blindspot	blush
blink'ered	blushed
bliss	blush'ing
bliss'ful	blus'ter
bliss'fulness	blus'tered
blis'ter	blus'tering
blis'tered	blus'tery
blis'tering	board
blithe	board'ed
blitz	board'er
bliz'zard	board'ing
block	board'ing-
blockade'	house
blockad'ed	boast
blockad'ing	boast'ed
blocked	boast'ful
block'head	boast'fulness
blond, blonde	boast'ing
blood	boat
blood'-group	boat'house
blood'shed	boat'swain
bloom	bob
bloomed	bobbed
blos'som	bob'sleigh
blos'somed	bod'ily
blot	bod'y
blotch	bod'y-*guard*
blot'ter	boff'in
blouse	bo'gus
blow	Bohe'mian
blow'ing	boil
blow'lamp	boiled
blown	boil'er
blue	bois'terous
blue'berry	bois'terously
blue'-chip	bold
bluff	bold'er

bold'ly	bored
bold'ness	bore'dom
Bol'shevik	bo'ring
bol'ster	born
bol'stered	borne
bol'stering	bor'ough
bolt	bor'row
bolt'ed	bor'rowed
bomb	bor'rower
bom'bard, n.	bor'rowing
bombard', v.	bos'om
bombard'ed	boss
bombard'ing	bot'anist
bombard'ment	bot'any
bombast'ic	both
bomb'proof	both'er
bomb'shell	both'ered
bond	both'ering
bond'age	bot'tle
bond'ed	bot'tleneck
bond'holder	bot'tling
bone	bot'tom
bon'fire	boudoir'
bon'net	bough
bo'nus	bought
book	boul'der
book'binder	boul'evard
book'binding	bounce
book'case	bounced
book'-keeper	bounc'ing
book'-keeping	bound
book'let	bound'ary
book'seller	bound'ed
book'shelf	bound'ing
book'stall	bound'less
book'store	boun'tiful
book'worm	boun'ty
boom	bouquet'
boomed	bourgeois'
boon	bour'geois
boost	bout
boost'er	boutique'
boot	bow (part of
booth	violin; a
bor'der	weapon)
bor'dering	bow (part of a
bor'derline	ship; to bend
bore	the body)

bowed	
bow'els	
bow'er	
bow'ing	
bowl	
bowled	
bowl'er	
bow'line	
box	
boxed	
box'er	
box'-office	
boy	
boy'cott	
boy'hood	
boy'ish	
boy'ishly	
bra	
brace	
braced	
brace'let	
bra'ces	
brack'et	
brack'eted	
brag	
bragged	
braid	
braid'ed	
braid'ing	
Braille	
brain	
brain'less	
brain'wash	
brain'wave	
brake	
branch	
branch'ing	
brand	
brand'ed	
bran'dish	
bran'dished	
bran'dy	
brass	
brass'erie	
brass'ière	
brava'do	
brave	
brave'ly	

brav'ery	
brav'est	
brawl	
brawled	
brawn	
bra'zen	
Brazil'ian	
breach	
bread	
breadth	
bread'winner	
break	
break'able	
break'age	
break'down	
break'fast	
break'ing	
break'neck	
break'water	
breast	
breath	
breathe	
breath'less	
bred	
breech	
breed	
breed'er	
breed'ing	
breeze	
breez'y	
breth'ren	
brev'ity	
brew	
brew'ing	
bribe	
bribed	
brib'ery	
brick	
brick'layer	
brick'work	
brick'yard	
bri'dal	
bride	
bridge	
bri'dle	
bri'dled	
brief	
brief'est	

brief'ly	bronzed
brigade'	bronz'ing
brigadier'	brooch
brig'and	brood
bright	brood'ed
bright'en	brood'ing
bright'er	brook
bright'ly	broom
bright'ness	broth
bril'liance	broth'er
bril'liancy	broth'erhood *or*
bril'liant	broth'er-in-law
bril'liantly	brought
brim	brow
brim'ful	brown
brine	bruise
bring	bruised
brink	brunette'
brisk	brunt
bris'tle	brush
bris'tled	brushed
Britan'nic	brush'wood
Brit'ish	brusque
brit'tle	bru'tal
brit'tleness	brutal'ity
broach	bru'tally
broach'ing	brute
broad	bub'ble
broad'cast	bub'bled
broad'caster	buck
broad'casting	buck'et
broad'en	buc'kle
broad'er	buck'ram
broad'ly	buck'wheat
broad'mind'ed	bucol'ic
brocade'	bud
brocad'ed	bud'ding
bro'chure	budg'erigar'
brogue	budg'et
broke	budg'eting
bro'ken	buff
brok'en-	buf'falo
heart'ed	buf'fet
bro'ker	buf'feted
bro'mide	bug'bear
bron'chial	bug'gy
bronchi'tis	bu'gle
bronze	bu'gler

build	
build′er	
build′ing	
built	
bulb	
bulge	
bulk	
bulk′y	
bull	
bull′doze	
bull′dozer	
bul′let	
bul′letin	
bul′let-proof	
bul′lied	
bul′lion	
bul′lock	
bul′ly	
bul′lying	
bul′wark	
bump	
bumped	
bump′er	
bump′ing	
bump′tious	
bump′tious- ness	
bun	
bunch	
bun′dle	
bun′galow	
bun′gle	
bunk	
bunk′er	
buoy	
buoy′ancy	
buoy′ant	
buoy′antly	
buoyed	
bur′den	
bur′densome	
bureau′	
bur′eaucrat	
bureaucrat′ic	
burg	
burg′lar	

burg′lary	
bur′ial	
bur′ied	
burlesque′	
bur′ly	
burn	
burned	
burn′er	
burn′ing	
burnt	
bur′row	
bur′rowed	
bur′rowing	
burst	
burst′ing	
bur′y	
bur′ying	
bus	
bush	
bush′el	
bus′ier	
bus′iest	
bus′ily	
bus′iness	
bus′inesslike	
bus′inessman′	
bust	
bus′tle	
bus′tled	
bus′y	
but	
butch′er	
but′ler	
butt	
butt′ed	
but′ter	
but′ton	
but′tonhole	
buy	
buy′er	
buy′ing	
buzz	
by, bye	
by′pass	
by′-prod′uct	
by′stander	
by′*word*	

C

cab
cab'bage
cab'in
cab'inet
ca'ble
ca'blegram
cack'le
cadet'
Caesa'rean
ca'fé
cafete'ria
cage
cajole'
cake
caked
calam'itous
calam'ity
cal'culable
cal'culate
cal'culated
cal'culating
calcula'tion
Caledo'nian
cal'endar,
    cal'ender
cal'endered
calf
cal'ibre,
    cal'iber
cal'ico
calk, caulk
call
called
call'er
call'-girl
*call'*ing
cal'lous
cal'lousness
calm
calmed

calm'er
calm'ly
cal'orie
calum'niate
cal'umny
calyp'so
camaraderie
cam'ber
cam'bric
came
cam'el
cam'eo
cam'era
cam'ouflage
camp
campaign'
camp'-bed
camped
cam'phor
cam'phorated
camp'ing
cam'pus
can
can
Cana'dian
canal'
can'apé
cana'ry
can'cel
cancella'tion
can'celled
can'celling
can'cer
can'did
can'didacy
can'didate
can'didly
can'dle
can'dlestick

31

can'dour, can'dor	capri'cious
can'dy	capsize'
cane	capsized'
can'ine	cap'stan
can'ister	cap'sule
can'ker	cap'tain
can'kered	cap'tion
canned	cap'tivate
can'nery	cap'tivated
can'ning	captiva'tion
can'non	cap'tive
can'not	captiv'ity
canoe'	cap'tor
can'on	cap'ture
cañ'on	cap'tured
can'opy	car
cant	car'amel
cantan'kerous	car'at
canteen'	car'avan
can'ter	car'bide
can'tered	carbohy'drate
can'ton	carbol'ic
can'vas, *adj., n.*	car'bon
can'vass, *v.*	carbon'ic
can'vassed	car'bonizer
can'vasser	car'burate
can'yon	car'burettor, car'buretter
cap	car'cass
capabil'ity	carcinogen'ic
ca'pable	card
ca'pably	card'board
capa'cious	car'diac
capac'itance	car'digan
capac'itor	car'dinal
capac'ity	card'-in'dex
cape	car'diogram
cap'ital	car'diograph
cap'italism	*care*
cap'italist	*cared*
capitalis'tic	career'
capitaliza'tion	career'ist
cap'italize	*care'*free
Cap'itol	*care'*ful
capit'ulate	*care'*fully
capitula'tion	*care'*less
caprice'	*care'*lessness
	caress'

caressed'		cas'tigate	
car'et		castiga'tion	
care'worn		cast'ing	
car'go		cast'-iron	
car'icature		cas'tle	
car'icatured		cas'tor	
car'ing		cas'ual	
car'mine		cas'ually	
carna'tion		cas'uals	
car'nival		cas'ualty	
carn'ivore		cat	
carniv'orous		cat'aclysm	
car'ol		cat'alogue	
carp		cat'apult	
car'penter		cat'aract	
car'pentry		catarrh'	
car'pet		catarrh'al	
car'riage		catas'trophe	
car'ried		catastroph'ic	
car'rier		catch	
car'rot		catch'-phrase	
car'ry		catch'ing	
car'rying		cat'echism	
cart		categor'ical	
cart'age		cat'egory	
carte blanche'		ca'ter	
cart'ed		ca'tering	
car'ton		cat'erpillar	
cartoon'		cathe'dral	
cartoon'ist		Cath'olic,	
car'tridge		cath'olic	
carve		Cathol'icism	
carved		cat'tle	
carv'er		caught	
carv'ing		caul'dron	
cascade'		cau'liflower	
case		caulk	
cash		cause	
cashed		caused	
cashier'		caus'ing	
cash'ing		caus'tic	
cash'mere		cau'terize	
cash'-register		cau'tion	
cask		cau'tionary	
cas'ket		cau'tioned	
cassette		cau'tioning	
cast			
caste			

cau'tious	cen'tigrade
cau'tiously	cen'tral
cavalcade'	centraliza'tion
cavalier'	cen'tralize
cav'alry	cen'tralized
cave	cen'tre
cav'ern	cen'tred
cav'il	cen'turing
cav'ity	cen'tury
cease	ceram'ics
ceased	ce'real
cease'less	ceremo'nial
cease'lessly	ceremo'nious
ceas'ing	cer'emony
ce'dar	cer'tain
cede	cer'tainly
ce'ded	cer'tainty
ceil'ing	cert'ifiable
cel'ebrate	*certif'icate*
cel'ebrated	certif'icated
cel'ebrating	certifica'tion
celebra'tion	cer'tified
celeb'rity	cer'tify
celer'ity	cessa'tion
cel'ery	chafe
celes'tial	chafed
cel'ibacy	chaff
cel'ibate	cha'fing
cell	chagrin'
cel'lar	chain
cell'ophane	*chair*
cel'luloid	*chair*'man
cel'lulose	*chair*'manship
Celt'ic	chalk
cement'	chal'lenge
cement'ed	chal'lenged
cement'ing	chal'lenger
cem'etery	cham'ber
cen'otaph	cham'berlain
cen'sor	chame'leon
cen'sorship	champagne'
cen'sure	cham'pion
cen'sured	cham'pioned
cen'suring	cham'pionship
cen'sus	chance
cen'suses	chanced
cent	chan'cellor
cen'tenary	chan'cery

change	
change'able	
changed	
chan'ging	
chan'nel	
chant	
chant'ed	
cha'os	
chaot'ic	
chap	
chap'el	
chap'eron	
chap'lain	
chap'ter	
char	
char'-à-banc	
char'acter	
characteris'tic	
characteris'tic-	
ally	
char'coal	
charge	
charge'able	
charged	
charg'ing	
char'itable	
char'ity	
char'la'dy	
char'latan	
charm	
charm'ing	
charred	
chart	
char'ter	
char'tered	
char'woman	
cha'ry	
chase	
chased	
chasm	
chas'sis	
chaste	
chastise'	
chastised'	
chas'tisement	
chastis'ing	
chas'tity	
chat	

chat'ted	
chat'tel	
chat'ter	
chauf'feur	
cheap	
cheap'en	
cheap'ly	
cheat	
cheat'ed	
cheat'ing	
check	
check'ing	
check'-up	
cheek	
cheer	
cheered	
cheer'ful	
cheer'fulness	
cheer'ing	
cheer'less	
cheese	
chef	
chem'ical	
chem'ist	
chem'istry	
cheque	
cheque'-book	
cher'ish	
cher'ished	
cher'ry	
ches'nut	
chess	
chest	
chest'nut	
chew	
chewed	
chew'ing	
chic	
chick'en	
chic'ory	
chief	
chief'ly	
chil'blain	
child	
child'hood	
child'ish	
child'ishly	
chil'dren	

chill	Christ'mas
chilled	chromat'ic
chime	chrome
chimed	chro'mium
chim'ney	chrom'osome
chimpan'zee	chron'ic
chin	chron'icle
chi'na	chronolog'-
Chinese'	ical-ly
chintz	chrysan'the-
chip	mum
chirop'odist	chum
chirop'ody	church
chiroprac'tor	church'*yard*
chirp	churl'ish
chis'el	churl'ishly
chis'el(l)er	churn
chiv'alrous	chute
chiv'alry	chut'ney
chlor'inate	ci'der
chlo'roform	cigar'
	cigarette'
choc'olate	cinch
choice	cin'der
choi'cest	cin'e
choir	cine-cam'era
choke	cin'ema
chol'era	cinemat'o-
choose	graph
choos'ing	cin'namon
chop	ci'pher
chopped	cir'ca
chop'per	cir'cle
chop'ping	cir'cuit
cho'ral	cir'cuited
chord	circu'itous
chore	cir'cular
choreog'rapher	circulariza'tion
choreog'raphy	cir'cularize
cho'rus	cir'culate
chose	cir'culated
chos'en	cir'culating
Christ	circula'tion
chris'ten	circum'ference
Chris'tendom	circumscribe'
chris'tened	circumscribed'
Chris'tian	cir'cumspect
Christian'ity	

circumspec'-
tion
cir'cumstance
cir'cumstanced
circumstan'tial
circumvent'
cir'cus
cis'tern
cit'adel
cita'tion
cite
ci'ted
cit'izen
cit'izenship
cit'rus
cit'y
civ'ic
civ'il
civil'ian
civil'ity
civiliza'tion
civ'ilize
civ'ilized
clad
claim
claim'ant
claimed
claim'ing
clam'ber
clam'bered
clam'our,
clam'or
clam'orous
clamp
clandes'tine
clang
clanged
clap
clar'ify
clash
clashed
clasp
class
classed
clas'sic
clas'sical
classifica'tion
classifi'able

clas'sify
class'room
clat'ter
clause
claustrophob'ia
claw
clawed
clay
clean
cleaned
clean'er
clean'est
clean'ing
clean'liness
clean'ly, *adj.*
clean'ly, *adv.*
cleanse
cleans'er
cleans'ing
clear
clear'ance
cleared
clear'er
clear'est
clear'ing
clear'ing-house
clear'ly
clear'ness
clear'-sighted
clear'way
clem'ency
clench
clench'ing
cler'gy
cler'gyman
cler'ic
cler'ical
clerk
clerk'ship
clev'er
clew
cliché
click
cli'ent
clientele'
cliff
cli'mate

climat'ic	clus'ter
cli'max	clus'tered
climb	clus'tering
climbed	clutch
climb'er	clutch'ing
climb'ing	coach
clinch	coach'ing
cling	coach'work
cling'ing	coal
clin'ic	coal'face
clinic'ian	coal'-gas
clink	coali'tion
clink'er	coal'-tar
clip	coarse
clipped	coars'en
clip'ping	coarse'ness
clique	coars'est
cloak	coast
clock	coast'al
clock'work	coast'-guard
clog	coast'ing
clogged	coast'line
clois'ter	coat
close	coat'ed
closed	coax
close'ly	coax'ial
clos'est	cob'bler
clos'et	co'caine
close'up	cock
clo'sure	co'co
clot	co'coa
cloth	cocoon'
clothe	cod
cloth'ier	code
cloth'ing	cod'icil
cloud	cod'ify
cloud'burst	co'ed'
cloud'ed	coed'ucate
clo'ver	coeduca'tional
clo'verleaf	coerce'
clown	coer'cion
club	cof'fee
club'-house	cof'fer
clue	cof'fin
clump	cog
clum'sily	co'gency
clum'sy	co'gent
clung	

cog'itate	collide'
cogita'tion	colli'ded
co'gnac	colli'ding
cohere'	col'lier
coher'ence	col'liery
coher'ency	colli'sion
coher'ent	collo'quial
cohe'sion	collo'quialism
cohe'sive	collu'sion
coiffeuse'	co'lon
coiffure	col'onel
coif'fured	colo'nial
coil	col'onist
coin	coloniza'tion
coin'age	col'onize
coincide'	col'ony
coin'cidence	col'or, col'our
coke	col'ored,
cold	col'oured
cold'er	col'ourful
cold'est	col'oring,
cold'-hearted	col'ouring
cold'ly	colos'sal
cold'ness	colt
collab'orate	Colum'bian
collabora'tion	col'umn
collab'orator	col'umnist
collage'	comb
collapse'	com'bat
collapsed'	com'batant
collaps'ible	combed
col'lar	combina'tion
col'lared	combine'
collate'	combin'ing
colla'ted	combus'tible
collat'eral	combus'tion
col'league	*come*
col'lect, *n.*	come'dian
	com'edy
collect', *v.*	comely
collect'ed	com'et
collec'tion	com'fort
collect'ive	com'fortable
collect'ively	com'forted
collect'or	com'forter
col'lege	com'forting
colle'giate	com'ic
	com'ical

*com'*ing	commo'tion
command'	{com'mune, *n.*
command'ed	{commune', *v.*
command'er	commu'nicate
command'-ment	commu'ni-cated
commem'orate	communica'tion
commem'-orated	commun'ion
commemora'tion	commu'niqué
commence'	com'munism
commenced'	com'munist
commence'-ment	commu'nity
commend'	commuta'tion
commend'able	commute'
commenda'-tion	{com'pact, *n.*
commen'-datory	{compact', *v.,adj.*
commend'ed	compan'ion
commen'surate	compan'ion-ship
com'ment	com'pany
com'mentary	com'parable
com'mented	compar'ative
com'merce	compar'atively
commer'cial	compare'
commer'cialize	compared'
commer'cially	compar'ing
commissar'	compar'ison
commissa'riat	compart'ment
commis'sion	com'pass
commis'sioner	compas'sion
commit'	compas'sionate
commit'ment	compatibil'ity
commit'ted	compat'ible
commit'tee	compat'riot
commit'ting	compel'
commo'dious	compelled'
commod'ity	compen'dium
com'mon	com'pensate
com'moner	com'pensated
com'monest	com'pensating
com'monly	compensa'tion
com'monplace	compete'
com'mon-wealth	compet'ed
	com'petence
	com'petent
	com'petently
	compet'ing

competi'tion	compo'sure
compet'itive	com'pound, *n.*
compet'itor	compound', *v.*
compila'tion	
compile'	compound'ed
compiled'	comprehend'
compi'ler	comprehend'ed
compla'cency	comprehend'-
compla'cent	ing
compla'cently	comprehen'-
complain'	sible
complain'ant	comprehen'-
complained'	sion
complain'ing	comprehen'-
complaint'	sive
complais'ant	com'press, *n.*
com'plement	compress', *v.*
complement'-	compressed'
ary	compres'sion
complete'	comprise'
comple'ted	comprised'
complete'ly	com'promise
complete'ness	com'promised
complet'ing	comptrol'ler
comple'tion	compul'sion
com'plex	compul'sorily
complex'ion	compul'sory
complex'ity	compunc'tion
compli'ance	computa'tion
compli'ant	compute'
com'plicate	compu'ter
com'plicated	com'rade
complica'tion	con'cave
complic'ity	conceal'
complied'	concealed'
com'pliment	conceal'ment
compliment'-	concede'
ary	conce'ded
com'plimented	conceit'
comply'	conceit'ed
comply'ing	conceiv'able
compo'nent	conceive'
compose'	conceived'
composed'	con'centrate
compo'ser	con'centrated
com'posite	con'centrating
composi'tion	concentra'tion
compos'itor	

concep'tion		condescen'sion	
concern'		condi'tion	
concerned'		condi'tional	
concern'ing		condole'	
con'cert, *n.*		condo'lence	
concert', *v.*		condomin'ium	
concer'to		condu'cive	
conces'sion		con'duct, *n.*	
concessionnaire'		conduct', *v.*	
concil'iate		conduct'ed	
concil'iated		conduct'or	
concilia'tion		con'duit	
concise'		cone	
concise'ly		confec'tion	
concise'ness		confec'tioner	
conclude'		confec'tionery	
conclu'ded		confed'erate	
conclu'ding		confedera'tion	
conclu'sion		confer'	
conclu'sive		con'ference	
conclu'sively		conferred'	
concoct'		confess'	
concoct'ed		confessed'	
concoct'ing		confes'sion	
concoc'tion		confide'	
concom'itant		confi'ded	
con'cord		con'fidence	
con'course		con'fident	
con'crete		confiden'tial	
concur'		con'fidently	
concurred'		confine'	
concur'rence		confined'	
concur'rent		confine'ment	
concur'rently		confirm'	
concus'sion		confirma'tion	
condemn'		confirmed'	
condemna'tion		con'fiscate	
condemned'		con'fiscated	
condemn'ing		confisca'tion	
condensa'tion		conflagra'tion	
condense'		con'flict, *n.*	
condensed'		conflict', *v.*	
condens'er		conflict'ed	
condens'ing		conflict'ing	
condescend'		conform'	
condescend'ed		conformed'	
condescend'ing		conform'ity	
		confound'	

confound'ed
confront'
confront'ed
confront'ing
confuse'
confused'
confu'sion
congeal'
conge'nial
congen'ially
congen'ital
conges'tion
conglomera'-
    tion
congrat'ulate
congrat'ulated
congratula'tion
con'gregate
con'gregated
con'gregating
congrega'tion
congrega'-
    tional
con'gress
congres'sional
con'gressmen
conjec'ture
conjec'tured
con'jugal
conjunc'tion
conjure'
con'jure
conjured'
con'jured
con'jurer
connect'
connect'ed
connec'tion,
    connex'ion
conni'vance
connive'
con'quer
con'quered
con'queror
con'quest
con'science
conscien'tious

conscien'-
    tiously
con'scious
con'sciously
con'sciousness
⎰con'script,
⎱ *adj.*
⎰conscript', *v.*
conscrip'tion
con'secrate
con'secrated
consecra'tion
consec'utive
consec'utively
consen'sus
consent'
consent'ed
con'sequence
con'sequent
con'sequently
conserva'tion
conserv'ative
conserv'atively
conserve'
consid'er
consid'erable
consid'erably
consid'erate
consid'erately
considera'tion
consid'ered
consid'ering
consign'
consigned'
consignee'
consign'er
consign'ment
consignor'
consist'
consist'ed
consist'ency
consist'ent
consist'ently
consist'ing
consola'tion
console'
consoled'
consol'idate

consol'idated	consume'
consol'idating	consumed'
consolida'tion	consu'mer
con'sonant	consum'mate
consonan'tal	consumma'-
con'sort, n.	tion
consort', v.	consump'tion
consort'ed	consump'tive
consor'tium	con'tact
conspic'uous	conta'gion
conspic'uously	conta'gious
conspir'acy	contain'
conspir'ator	contained'
conspire'	contain'er
conspired'	contam'inate
con'stable	contam'inated
constab'ulary	contam'inat-
con'stant	ing
con'stantly	contamina'-
consterna'tion	tion
constit'uency	con'template
constit'uent	con'templated
con'stitute	con'templating
con'stituted	contempla'tion
con'stituting	contempora'-
constitu'tion	neous
constitu'tional	contem'porary
constitu'tion-	contempt'
ally	contempt'ible
constrain'	contemp'tuous
constraint'	contemp'tu-
constrict'	ously
constrict'ed	contend'
constric'tion	contend'ed
construct'	contend'er
construct'ed	con'tent,
construc'tion	content'
construct'ive	content'ed
construct'ively	content'edly
con'strue	conten'tion
con'strued	*content'ment*
con'sul	con'tents,
con'sular	contents'
consult'	{con'test, n.
consult'ant	{contest', v.
consulta'tion	contest'ant
consult'ed	contest'ed
consult'ing	contest'ing

con'text	
contig'uous	
con'tinent	
continen'tal	
contin'gency	
contin'gent	
contin'gently	
contin'ual	
contin'ually	
contin'uance	
continua'tion	
contin'ue	
contin'ued	
contin'uing	
continu'ity	
contin'uous	
contin'uously	
contin'uum	
con'tour	
con'tra	
con'traband	
contracep'tion	
contracep'tive	
{con'tract, *n.*	
{contract', *v.*	
contract'ed	
contrac'tion	
contract'or	
contradict'	
contradict'ed	
contradic'tion	
contradict'ory	
contrap'tion	
con'trary	
{con'trast, *n.*	
{contrast', *v.*	
contrast'ed	
contrast'ing	
contravene'	
contraven'tion	
contrib'ute	
contrib'uted	
contrib'uting	
contribu'tion	
contrib'utor	
contrib'utory	
contri'vance	
contrive'	

control'	
control'lable	
controlled'	
control'ler	
controver'sial	or
con'troversy	or
conun'drum	
conurba'tion	
convales'cence	
convales'cent	
convec'tor	
convene'	
convened'	
conve'nience	
conve'nient	
conve'niently	
con'vent	
conven'tion	
conven'tional	
con'versant	
conversa'tion	
conversa'tional	
{con'verse,	
{ *n., adj.*	
{converse', *v.*	
conversed'	
con'versely	
conver'sion	
{con'vert, *n.*	
{convert', *v.*	
convert'ed	
convert'ible	
con'vex	
convey'	
convey'ance	
convey'or	
{con'vict, *n.*	
{convict', *v.*	
convict'ed	
convict'ing	
convic'tion	
convince'	
convinced'	
convin'cing	
conviv'ial	

con'voy, *n.*
convoy', *v.*
convulse'
convul'sion
convul'sive
cook
cooked
cook'er
cook'ery
cook'ing
cool
cool'ant
cooled
cool'er
cool'est
coo'lie
cool'ly
co-op'erate
co-op'erated
co-op'erating
co-opera'tion
co-op'erative
co-op'erator
co-opt'
co-or'dinate, *v.*
co-or'dinate, *n.a.*
co-ordina'tion
co-ord'inator
copart'nership
cope
cop'ied
co'-pi'lot
co'ping
co'pious
cop'per
cop'y
cop'yholder
cop'ying
cop'yright
copy-*wri'ter*
cor'al
cord
cor'dial
cordial'ity
cor'don
cor'duroy

core
cork
cork'screw
corn
cor'ner
cor'nice
corol'lary
corona'tion
cor'oner
cor'porate
corpora'tion
corps
corpse
cor'pulence
cor'pulency
cor'pulent
cor'puscle
correct'
correct'ed
correct'ing
correc'tion
correct'ive
correct'ly
correct'ness
cor'relate
cor'related
correla'tion
correspond'
correspond'ed
correspond'-
  ence
correspond'ent
correspond'ing
cor'ridor
corrob'orate
corrob'orated
corrob'orating
corrobora'tion
corrob'orative
corrob'oratory
corrode'
corro'ded
corro'sion
corro'sive
corrupt'
corrup'tion
cort'isone
co'sily

cosmet'ic	count'ess
cos'monaut	count'ing
cosmop'olis	count'ing-
cosmopol'itan	house
cost	count'less
cost'liness	count'ry
cost'ly	count'ryman
cos'tume	coun'tryside
co'sy	count'y
co'terie	coupé'
cot'tage	coup'le
cot'ton	cou'pon
couch	cour'age
cough	coura'geous
coughed	course
cough'ing	coursed
could	court
coun'cil	court'eous
coun'cillor,	court'esy
coun'cilor	court-mar'tial
coun'sel	cous'in
coun'selled,	couture'
coun'seled	couturier'
coun'sellor,	
coun'selor	cov'enant
count	cov'er
count'ed	cov'er-charge
coun'tenance	cov'ered
count'er	cov'ering
counteract'	cov'et
counteract'ed	cov'etous
counter-	cow
bal'ance	cow'ard
counter-	cow'ardice
bal'anced	coy
counterbal'-	co'zily
ancing	co'zy
coun'terblast	crab
count'erclaim	crack
	cracked
count'erfeit	cra'dle
count'erfeited	craft
count'erfeiter	craft'ily
count'erfoil	craft'iness
countermand'	crafts'man
counter-	craft'y
mand'ed	cram
count'erpart	cramp

cramped		cres'cent	
cran'berry		crest	
crane		cretonne'	
crank		crev'ice	
crash		crew	
crashed		crib	
crash'-landing		crick'et	
crate		crick'eter	
cra'ter		cried	
crave		crime	
craved		crim'inal	
cra'ving		crim'son	
crawl		crip'ple	
crawled		cri'sis	
cray'on		crisp	
craze		crite'rion	
crazed		crit'ic	
cra'zy		crit'ical	
creak		crit'icism	
creaked		crit'icize	
cream		crit'icized	
crease		cro'chet	
creased		cro'cheted	
create'		crock'ery	
crea'ted		crook	
crea'tion		crook'ed	
crea'tive		crop	
creativ'ity		crop'per	
crea'tor		croquette'	
crea'ture		cross	
cre'dence		crossed	
creden'tial		*cross-exam-*	
credibil'ity		*ina'tion*	
cred'ible		*cross-exam'-*	
cred'it		*ine-d*	
cred'itable		*cross-exam'-*	
cred'ited		*ining*	
cred'iting		cross'-	
cred'itor		ref'erence	
credu'lity		cross'roads	
cred'ulous		cross'-sec'tion	
creed		cross'*word*	
creek		crowd	
creep		crowd'ed	
creep'ing		crowd'ing	
cre'ole		crown	
crêpe		crowned	
crept		cru'cial	

cru'cifix	cu'mulative
crucifix'ion	Cunard'er
cru'cify	cun'ning
crude	cun'ningly
cru'dity	cup
cru'el	cup'board
cru'elly	cu'pro-nick'el
cru'elty	cur'able
cru'et	curb
cruise	cure
cruis'er	cured
crumb	cur'ing
crum'ble	cu'rio
crum'ple	curios'ity
crusade'	cu'rious
crush	cu'riously
crushed	curl
crust	curled
crust'ed	curl'y
crutch	cur'rant
crux	cur'rency
cry	cur'rent
cry'ing	cur'rently
crypt'ic	curric'ula
crys'tal	curric'ulum
crys'tallize	curse
Cu'ban	cursed
cube	curs'ed
cu'bic	cur'sive
cu'cumber	curs'or
cue	cur'sorily
cuff	cur'sory
cul'minate	curt
cul'minated	curtail'
culmina'tion	curtailed
culottes'	curtail'ment
cul'pable	cur'tain
cul'prit	curt'ly
cul'tivate	curv'ature
cul'tivated	curve
cultiva'tion	curved
cul'tural	curv'ing
cul'ture	cush'ion
cul'tured	cus'tard
cul'vert	custo'dian
cum'bersome	cus'tody
cum'brous	cus'tom

cus'tomarily
cus'tomary

cus'tomer
cus'tom-house
cus'toms
cut
cute
cu'test
cut'lery
cut'ter
cybernet'ics
cy'cle

cyc'lical
cy'clist
cy'clone
cyclop(a)e'dia
cy'clotron
cyl'inder
cylin'drical
cyn'ic
cyn'ical
cyn'icism
cyn'osure
cy'pher
cy'press

D

dab'ble		dash	
dad		dash'board	
dad'dy		dashed	
dai'ly		das'tardly	
dain'ty		da'ta	
dai'ry		date	
da'is		da'ted	
dai'sy		date'-line	
dam		daugh'ter	
dam'age		daunt	
dam'aged		daunt'ed	
dam'aging		daunt'less	
dam'ask		dav'it	
dame		dawn	
damn		day	
damp		day'break	
damp'en		day'light	
damp'er		day'time	
damp'ness		daze	
dance		daz'zle	
danced		daz'zled	
dan'cer		dead	
dan'cing		dead'beat	
dan'dy		dead'en	
dan'ger		dead'ened	
dan'gerous		dead'lock	
dan'gerously		deaf	
Da'nish		deaf'-aid	
dare		deaf'en	
dared		deaf'ened	
dar'ing		deal	
dar'ingly		deal'er	
dark		dealt	
dark'en		dean	
dark'er		*dear*	
dar'ling		*dear'er*	
darn		*dear'est*	
darned		dearth	
dart		death	
dart'ed		débâc'le	

debag'		dec'imal	
debar'		dec'imate	
debarred'		decima'tion	
debar'ring		deci'pher	
debase'		deci'phered	
debased'		deci'sion	
deba'table		deci'sive	
debate'		deci'sively	
deba'ted		deck	
deba'ting		declara'tion	or
deben'ture		declare'	
debil'ity		declared'	
deb'it		declar'ing	
deb'ited		declen'sion	
deb'iting		decline'	
debonair'		decli'ning	
débris'		decliv'ity	
debt		declutch'	
debt'or		decode'	
debunk'		decompose'	
début'		decomposed'	
déb'utant		decomposi'tion	
déb'utante		decompress'	
dec'ade		decontam'inate	
dec'adence		decontrol'	
decay'		dec'orate	
decayed'		dec'orated	
decay'ing		decora'tion	
decease'		dec'orative	
deceased'		dec'orator	
deceit'		deco'rous	
deceit'ful		deco'rum	
deceit'fulness		de'coy	
deceive'		decoyed'	
decel'erate		decoy'ing	
Decem'ber		decrease'	
de'cency		decreased'	
de'cent		decree'	
de'cently		decreed'	
decentraliza'tion		decrep'it	
decen'tralize		decried'	
decep'tion		decry'	
decep'tive		ded'icate	
de'cibel		ded'icated	
decide'		dedica'tion	
deci'ded		deduce'	
deci'dedly		deduced'	

deduct'	defi'ciency
deduct'ed	defi'cient
deduct'ing	defi'ciently
deduc'tion	def'icit
deduct'ive	defied'
deed	define'
deem	defined'
deemed	def'inite
deep	def'initely
deep'en	defini'tion
deep'er	deflate'
deep'est	defla'tion
deep'ly	deflect'
deer	deflect'ed
deface'	deform'
defaced'	deformed'
deface'ment	deform'ity
defal'cate	defraud'
defalca'tion	defraud'ed
defama'tion	defraud'ing
defam'atory	defray'
defame'	defrayed'
default'	defray'ing
default'ed	de'frost'
default'er	deft
default'ing	deft'ly
defeat'	defunct'
defeat'ed	defy'
defeat'ing	degen'erate,
defeat'ist	n. & a.
defect'	de'generate, v.
defect'ive	degen'erated
defence'	degrada'tion
defend'	degrade'
defend'ant	degra'ded
defend'ed	degree'
defen'sible	dehyd'rate
defen'sive	deign
defer'	deigned'
def'erence	de'ity
deferen'tial	deject'
defer'ment	deject'ed
deferred'	dejec'tion
defer'ring	delay'
defi'ance	delayed'
defi'ant	delay'ing
	del'egate, n.
	dele'gate, v.

del'egated	demoli'tion	
del'egating	demonetiza'-	
delega'tion	tion	
delete'	*dem'onstrate*	
delete'rious	*dem'onstrated*	
dele'tion	*dem'onstrating*	
delib'erate,	demonstra'tion	
adj.	dem'onstrative	
delib'erate, *v.*	dem'onstrator	
delibera'tion	demor'alize	
del'icacy	demor'alized	
del'icate	demor'alizing	
delicatess'en	demo'tion	
deli'cious	demur'	
delight'	demure'	
delight'ed	demur'rage	
delight'ful	demurred'	
delin'eate	demy'	
delinea'tion	deni'al	
delin'quency	denied'	
delin'quent	de'nim	
delir'ious	denom'inating	
delir'ium	(denomina'-	
deliv'erance	tion	
deliv'er-ed	(denomina'-	
deliv'ering	tional	
deliv'ery	denote'	
del'ta-wing	deno'ted	
delude'	deno'ting	
del'uge	denounce'	
delu'sion	denounced'	
delve	dense	
demand'	dense'ly	
demand'ed	den'sity	
demand'ing	dent	
demarca'tion	den'tal	
demean'our,	den'tifrice	
demean'or	den'tist	
demerar'a	den'tistry	
demo'bilize	denuncia'tion	
democ'racy	deny'	
dem'ocrat	deo'dorize	
democrat'ic	depart'	
demol'ish	depart'ed	
demol'ished	depart'ing	
	depart'ment	
	department'al	
	depar'ture	

depend'		derange'ment	
depend'able		der'elict	
depend'ed		derelic'tion	
depend'ence		deride'	
depend'ent		deri'ded	
deplete'		deri'sion	
deple'ted		deri'sive	
deple'ting		deriva'tion	
deple'tion		deriv'ative	or
deplor'able		derive'	
deplore'		deri'ving	
deplored'		descend'	
deplor'ing		descend'ant	
deport'		descend'ed	
deport'ed		descent'	
deport'ment		describe'	
depose'		descri'bing	
deposed'		descried'	
depos'it		*descrip'tion*	
depos'itary		descrip'tions	
depos'ited		descrip'tive	or
depos'iting		descry'	
deposi'tion		des'ecrate	
depos'itor		desecra'tion	
depos'itory		(des'ert, n., adj.	
dep'ot		desert', v.	
depraved'		desert'ed	
deprav'ity		desert'er	
dep'recate		desert'ing	
dep'recated		deser'tion	
depre'ciate	or	deserve'	
depre'ciated	or	deserv'edly	
depre'ciating	or	deserv'ing	
deprecia'tion		desidera'tum	
depress'		design'	
depressed'		des'ignate	
depres'sion		des'ignated	
depriva'tion		designa'tion	
deprive'		designed'	
depth		design'er	
deputa'tion		desirabil'ity	
depute'		desir'able	
depu'ted		desire'	
depu'ting		desired'	
dep'utize		desir'ing	
dep'uty		desir'ous	
derange'		desist'	

desist'ed	detec'tive
desist'ing	deten'tion
desk	deter'
des'olate, *adj.*	dete'riorate
des'olate, *v.*	dete'riorated
desola'tion	deteriora'tion
despair'	determina'tion
despaired'	deter'mine
despair'ing	deterred'
despair'ingly	deter'rent
despatch'	deter'ring
despera'do	detest'
des'perate	detest'able
despera'tion	detesta'tion
des'picable	detest'ed
despise'	detest'ing
despised'	det'onate
despite'	det'onated
despoil'	detona'tion
despoiled'	det'onator
despoil'er	detour'
despond'ency	detract'
despond'ent	detract'ed
des'pot	detract'or
dessert'	detrain'
destina'tion	det'riment
des'tine	detrimen'tal
des'tiny	deval'uate
des'titute	dev'astate
destitu'tion	dev'astated
destroy'	devasta'tion
destroy'er	devel'op
destroy'ing	devel'oped
destruc'tion	devel'oping
destruc'tive	devel'opment
destruc'tively	de'viate
des'ultory	de'viated
detach'	devia'tion
detach'ing	devia'tionist
detach'ment	device'
de'tail, *n.*	dev'il
detail', *v.*	de'vious
detailed'	devise'
detain'	devised'
detained'	devoid'
detect'	devolve'
detect'ed	devolved'
detec'tion	

devolv'ing	
devote'	
devo'ted	
devo'tedly	
devotee'	
devo'ting	
devo'tion	
devour'	
devoured'	
devour'ing	
devout'	
dew	
dexter'ity	
dex'terous	
diabe'tes	
diabol'ic	
diagnose'	
diagno'sis	
diag'onal	
di'agram	
di'al	
di'alect	
di'alling,	
di'aling	
di'alogue	
diam'eter	
diamet'ric	
diamet'rical	
di'amond	
di'aphragm	
di'arist	
di'ary	
{dic'tate, *n.*	
{dictate', *v.*	
dicta'ted	
dicta'ting	
dicta'tion	
dicta'tor	
dictato'rial	
dicta'torship	
dic'tion	
dic'tionary	
dic'tum	
did	
die	
died	
die'hard	
di'et	

di'etary	
di'eted	
dietet'ics	
di'eting	
dif'fer	
dif'fered	
{*dif*'ference	
{*dif*'ferent	
differen'tiate	
dif'ferently	
dif'ficult	
dif'ficulty	
dif'fidence	
dif'fident	
diffuse'	
diffused'	
diffu'sion	
dig	
di'gest, *n.*	
digest', *v.*	
digest'ed	
digest'ible	
digest'ing	
diges'tion	
digest'ive	
dig'it	
dig'nify	or
dig'nity	or
digress'	
digres'sion	
dike	
dilap'idate	or
dilap'idated	or
dilapida'tion	or
dilate'	
dil'atory	
dilem'ma	
dil'igence	
dil'igent	
dil'igently	
dilute'	
dilu'ted	
dilu'tion	
dim	

dimen'sion		disagree'ing	
dimin'ish		disagree'ment	
dimin'ished		disallow'	
diminu'tion		disappear'	
dimin'utive		disappear'ance	
dimmed		disappeared'	
din		disappear'ing	
dine		disappoint'	
di'ner		disappoint'ed	
din'gey,		disappoint'ing	
din'ghy		disappoint'-	
din'gy		ment	
di'ning		disapproba'-	
di'ning-room		tion	
din'ner		disapprov'al	
dint		disapprove'	
di'ocese		disapprov'ing	
di'ode		disarm'	
dip		disarm'ament	
di'phone		disarmed'	
diphthe'ria		disarrange'	
diph'thong		disarranged'	
diplo'ma		disas'ter	
diplo'macy		disas'trous	
dip'lomat		disas'trously	
diplomat'ic		disband'	
dire		disband'ed	
direct'		disbelief'	
direct'ed		disbelieve'	
direc'tion		disbelieved'	
direct'or		disburse'	
direct'orate		disbursed'	
direct'ory		disburse'ment	
dirn'dl		disc	
dirt		discard'	
dirt'y		discard'ed	
disabil'ity		discard'ing	
disa'ble		discern'	
disa'blement		discerned'	
disa'bling		discern'ible	
dis*advan'tage*		discern'ing	
dis*advanta'-*		discern'ment	
geous		*discharge'*	
dis*advanta'-*		*discharged'*	
geously		*discharg'*ing	
disagree'		disci'ple	
disagree'able		disciplina'rian	
disagreed'		dis'ciplinary	

dis'cipline
disc'-jock'ey
disclaim
disclose'
disclosed'
disclo'sure
discol'our,
  discol'or
discol'oured
discom'fit
discom'fited
discom'fiture
discom'fort
disconcert'
disconcert'ed
disconnect'
discontent'
discontent'ed
discontin'ue
discontin'ued
dis'cord
discord'ant
{dis'count, n.
{discount', v.
discount'ed
discour'age
discour'age-
  ment
discourse
discov'er
discov'ered
discov'ering
discov'ery
discred'it
discred'itable
discred'ited
discreet'
discrep'ancy
discre'tion
discrim'inate,
  a.
discrim'inate,
  v.
discuss'
discussed'
discus'sion
disdain'
disease'

diseased'
disembark'
disembarka'-
  tion
{disestab'lish
{disestab'-
  lished
{disestab'lish-
  ment
disfa'vour,
  disfa'vor
disfig'ure
disfig'urement
disfig'uring
disfran'chise
disgorge'
disgrace'
disgraced'
disgrace'ful
disgrace'fully
disgrun'tled
disguise'
disguised'
disgust'
disgust'ed
disgust'ing
dish
disheart'en
disheart'ened
disheart'ening
dishev'el
dishev'elled,
  dishev'eled
dishon'est
dishon'estly
dishon'esty
dishon'our,
  dishon'or
dishon'ourable
dishon'oured
disillu'sion
disincen'tive
disinclina'tion
disinclined'
disinfect'
disinfect'ant
disinfect'ed

disinher′it	dispersed′
disinher′itance	dispers′ing
disinher′ited	displace′
disin′tegrate	displaced′
disin′tegrated	displace′ment
disintegra′tion	display′
dis*in′terested*	displayed′
disjoint′ed	display′ing
dislike′	displease′
disliked′	displeased′
dis′locate	dis*pleas′ure*
dis′located	dispo′sal
dis′locating	dispose′
disloca′tion	disposed′
disloy′al	disposi′tion
dis′mal	dispossess′
disman′tle	dispossessed′
disman′tled	dis*propor′-*
dismay′	*tionate*
dismiss′	disprove′
dismiss′al	disput′able
dismissed′	dis′putant
dismiss′ing	dispute′
dismount′	dispu′ted
dismount′ed	dispu′ting
disobe′dience	disqualifica′-
disobe′dient	tion
disobey′	disqual′ify
disor′der	disqual′ifying
disor′derly	disregard′
dis*organiza′-*	disregard′ed
tion	disrep′utable
{disor′ganize	disrepute′
{disor′ganized	dis*respect′*
disown′	dis*respect′*ful
disowned′	disrup′tion
dispar′age	dis*satisfac′tion*
dispar′agement	dissat′isfied
	dissect′
dispatch′	dissec′tion
dispatch′ing	dissent′
dispen′sary	
dispensa′tion	dissim′ilar or
dispense′	
dispensed′	dis′sipate
dispen′sing	dis′sipated
dispers′al	dissipa′tion
disperse′	dissolu′tion
	dissolve′

dissuade′
dissua′ded
dis′tance
dis′tant
dis′tantly
distaste′
distaste′ful
distem′per
distil′, distill′
distilled′
distil′lery
distinct′
distinc′tion
distinct′ive
distinct′ively
distinct′ly
distin′guish
distin′guish-
    able
distin′guished
distin′guishing
distort′
distort′ed
distor′tion
distract′
distract′ed
distrac′tion
distrain′
distress′
distressed′
distress′ful
distrib′ute
distrib′uted
distrib′uter
distrib′uting
distribu′tion
distrib′utor
dis′trict
distrust′
distrust′ed
distrust′ful
disturb′
disturb′ance
disturbed′
disturb′ing
disuse′, *n.*
disuse′, *v.*
disused′

ditch
dit′to
divan′
dive
di′ver
diverge′
diver′gent
di′vers
diverse′
diver′sified
diver′sion
diver′sity
divert′
divert′ed
divide′
divi′ded
div′idend
divi′ding
divine′
divine′ly
divin′ity
divis′ible
divi′sion
divi′sional
divorce′
divorced′
divorcee′
divulge′
diz′zy
do
do′cile
dock
docker
dock′et
dock′yard
doc′tor
doc′trine
doc′ument
documen′tary
dod′derer
dodge
does, *v.*
dog
dog′ma
dogmat′ic
do′ing
dole
dole′ful

doll		down'cast	
dol'lar		down'fall	
domain'		down'hearted	
dome		down'hill	
domes'tic		down'pour	
domes'ticate		down'right	
domes'ticated		down'stairs	
dom'icile		down'wards	
dom'inant		doze	
dom'inate		dozed	
dom'inated		doz'en	
domina'tion		drab	
domineer'ing		drachm	
Domin'ican		draft	
domin'ion		draft'ed	
donate'		drag	
dona'ted		drain	
dona'ting		drain'age	
dona'tion		drake	
done		dram	
do'nor		dra'ma	
doo'dle		dramat'ic	
doom		dram'atist	
door		drank	
door'step		drape	
door'way		dra'per	
dope		dras'tic	
dor'mant		dras'tically	
dor'mitory		draught	
dose		draughts'man	
dot		draught'y	
dot'ted		draw	
dot'ting		drawee'	
doub'le		draw'er	
doubt		draw'ing	
doubt'ed		drawl	
doubt'ful		drawn	
doubt'fully		dray	
doubt'ing		dread	
doubt'ingly		dread'ed	
doubt'less		dread'ful	
doubts		dread'ing	
douche		dread'nought	
dough		dream	
dough'nut		dreamed	
dove'tail		dreamt'	
dove'tailed		drear'y	
down		dredge	

dredg'er		dubi'ety	
dregs		du'bious	
drench		du'cal	
Dres'den		duch'ess	
dress		duch'y	
dress'er		duck	
dress'maker		duc'tile	
dried		due	
dri'er		du'el	
drift		duet'	
drift'ed		dug	
drift'ing		duke	
drill		dull	
drilled		du'ly	
drink		dumb	
drink'er		dumbfound'	
drip		dumbfound'ed	
drive		dump	
driv'el		dun	
driv'en		dunce	
dri'ver		dune	
dri'ving		dun'ning	
driz'zle		duoden'al	
drom'edary		dupe	
drone		du'plex	
droop		du'plicate, n. & a.	
drop		du'plicate, v.	
dross		du'plicated	
drought		duplica'tion	
drouth		du'plicator	
drove		duplic'ity	
drown		durabil'ity	
drow'siness		du'rable	
drow'sy		dural'umin	
drudge		dura'tion	
drudg'ery		dur'ing	
drug		dusk	
drug'gist		dusk'y	
drum		dust	
drum'mer		dust'ed	
drunk		dust'er	
drunk'ard		Dutch	
drunk'en		du'tiable	
drunk'enness		du'tiful	
dry		du'ty	
dry'clean		dwarf	
dry'-rot			
du'al			

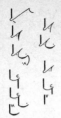

dwarfed	dy'er
dwell	dy'ing
dwell'er	dynam'ic
dwell'ing	dy'namite
dwell'ing-house	dy'namo
dwelt	dy'namotor
dwin'dle	dy'nasty
dwin'dled	dys'entery
dwin'dling	
dye	dyspep'sia
dye'ing	dyspep'tic

each	
ea'ger	
ea'gerly	
ea'gle	
ear	
ear'-ache	
earl	
ear'lier	
ear'liest	
ear'ly	
earn	
earned	
earn'er	
earn'est	
earn'estly	
earn'ing	
ear'-phone	
earth	
earth'en	
earth'enware	
earth'ly	
earth'quake	
ear'wig	
ease	
ea'sel	
eas'ier	
eas'iest	
eas'ily	
east	
East'er	
east'erly	
east'ern	
east'ward	
east'wards	
eas'y	
eas'y-chair	
eat	
eat'en	
eat'ing	
ebb	

ebbed	
ebb'tide	
eb'ony	
eccen'tric	
eccentric'ity	
ecclesias'tic	
ech'o	
ech'oed	
éc'lair	
eclipse'	
econom'ic	
econom'ical	
econom'ics	
econ'omist	
econ'omize	
econ'omy	
ec'stasy	
ecstat'ic	
ec'toplasm	
edge	
edg'y	
ed'ible	
e'dict	
edifica'tion	
ed'ifice	
ed'ified	
ed'ify	
ed'it	
ed'ited	
ed'iting	
edi'tion	
ed'itor	
edito'rial	
ed'itorship	
ed'ucate	
ed'ucated	
educa'tion	
educa'tional	
educa'tionalist	

educa'tionist	el'derly	
ed'ucator	el'dest	
eel	elect'	
ee'rie, ee'ry	elect'ed	
efface'	elec'tion	
efface'ment	elect'or	
effect'	elect'oral	
effect'ed	elect'orate	
effect'ing	*elec'tric*	
effect'ive	*elec'trical*	
effect'ively	*elec'trically*	
effects'	electri'cian	
effec'tual	*electric'ity*	
effem'inate	electrifica'tion	
effervesce'	elec'trified	
efferves'cent	elec'trify	
effica'cious	elec'trocute	
ef'ficacy	elec'trocuted	
[effi'ciency	electrol'ysis	
[effi'cient-ly	elec'tron	
ef'fort	electron'ic	
ef'fortless	electron'ics	
egg	el'egance	
Egyp'tian	el'egant	
eh	el'egantly	
ei'derdown	el'ement	
eight	elemen'tary	
eighteen	el'ephant	
eighteenth	el'evate	
eighth	el'evated	
eight'ieth	eleva'tion	
eight'y	el'evator	
ei'ther	elev'en	
ejac'ulate	elev'enth	
ejac'ulated	elic'it	
ejacula'tion	elic'ited	
eject'	eligibil'ity	
eject'ed	el'igible	
ejec'tion	elim'inate	
elab'orate, *adj.*	elim'inated	
elab'orate, *v.*	elim'inating	
elab'orately	elimina'tion	
elabora'tion	Elizabe'than	
elapse'	elm	
elas'tic	elocu'tion	
elastic'ity	elocu'tionist	
el'bow	e'longate	
el'der	e'longated	

elonga'tion
elope'
elope'ment
el'oquence
el'oquent
el'oquently
else
else'where
elu'cidate
elu'cidated
elucida'tion
elude'
elu'sive
elu'sively
ema'ciate
ema'ciated
em'anate
em'anating
eman'cipate
emancipa'tion
embalm'
embalmed'
embank'ment
embar'go
embark'
embarka'tion
embar'rass
embar'rass- ment
em'bassy
embed'
embed'ded
embel'lish
embel'lished
embel'lish- ment
embez'zle
embez'zled
embez'zlement
embez'zler
embit'ter
em'blem
embod'ied
embod'iment
embod'y
emboss'
embrace'

embroca'tion
embroid'er
embroid'ery
em'bryo
emend'
emenda'tion
em'erald
emerge'
emer'gency
em'ery
emet'ic
em'igrant
em'igrate
em'igrated
emigra'tion
em'inence
em'inent
em'inently
em'issary
emis'sion
emit'
emol'ument
emo'tion
emo'tional
em'pathy
em'peror
em'phasis
em'phasize
em'phasized
emphat'ic
emphat'ically
em'pire
empir'ical
employ'
employ'able
employee'
employees'
employ'er
employ'ing
employ'ment
empo'rium
empow'er
empow'ered
em'press
emp'tied
emp'ty
emp'tying
em'ulate

emula'tion
emul'sion
ena'ble
ena'bled
ena'bling
enact'
enact'ed
enact'ment
enam'el
enam'elled,
  enam'eled
enam'our,
  enam'or
enam'oured
encamp'
encamped'
encamp'ment
encase'
encased'
encash'ment
enchant'
enchant'ed
enchant'ment
encir'cle
enclose'
enclosed'
enclo'sure
encoun'ter
encoun'tered.
encount'ering
encour'age
encour'age-
  ment
encour'aging
encroach'
encroached'
encroach'ing
encroach'ment
encrust'
encrust'ed
encum'ber
encum'bered
encum'brance
encyclope'dia
end
endan'ger
endan'gering
endear'

endeav'our,
  endeav'or
end'ed
end'less
end'lessly
endorse'
endorse'ment
endow'
endowed'
endow'ment
endur'able
endur'ance
endure'
endured'
en'emy
energet'ic
en'ergy
en'ervate
en'ervated
enfold'
enfold'ed
enfold'ing
enforce'
enforced'
enforce'ment
enforc'ing
enfran'chise
enfran'chise-
  ment
engage'
engage'ment
engen'der
engen'dered
en'gine
engineer'
engineered'
engineer'ing
Eng'lish
Eng'lishman
*Eng'lish*woman
engrave'
engraved'
engra'ver
engra'ving
engross'
engrossed'
enhance'
enhanced'

enhance′ment		entertain′	
enhan′cing		entertained′	
enig′ma		entertain′er	
enigmat′ic		*entertain′ment*	
enjoin′		enthuse′	
enjoy′		*enthu′siasm*	
enjoy′able		enthu′siast	
enjoy′ment		*enthusias′tic*	
enlarge′		*enthusias′tic-*	
enlarged′		*ally*	
enlarge′ment		entice′	
enlar′ger		enticed′	
enlar′ging		entice′ment	
enlight′en		entire′	
enlight′ened		entire′ly	
enlight′enment		entire′ty	
enlist′		enti′tle	
enlist′ed		enti′tled	
enlist′ing		enti′tling	
enlist′ment		(en′trance, *n.*	
enli′ven		(entrance′, *v.*	
enli′vened		entranced′	
en′mity		entranc′ing	
enor′mity		en′trant	
enor′mous		entreat′	
enough′		entreat′ed	
enquire′		entreat′y	
enquired′		entrust′	
enquir′y		entrust′ed	
enrage′		entrust′ing	
enrich′		en′try	
enrol′, enroll′		enu′merate	
enrolled′		enu′merated	
enrol′ment		enumera′tion	
enshrine′		enun′ciate	
en′sign		enun′ciated	
ensue′		enuncia′tion	
ensued′		envel′op	
ensu′ing		en′velope	
ensure′		en′viable	
entail′		en′vied	
entailed′		en′vious	
entan′gle		envi′ronment	
entan′gled		envis′age	
entan′glement		en′voy	
en′ter		en′vy	
en′tered		en′zyme	
en′terprise		ep′ic	

epicen'tre		erra'ta	
epidem'ic		errat'ic	
ep'ilogue		erra'tum	
epis'copal	*or*	erred	
ep'isode		err'ing	
epis'tle		erro'neous	
ep'itaph		erro'neously	
ep'ithet		er'ror	
epit'ome		erst'while	
ep'och		er'udite	
e'quable		erudi'tion	
e'qual		erup'tion	
equalitar'ian		es'calator	
equal'ity	*or*	escape'	
equaliza'tion		eschew'	
e'qualize		eschewed'	
e'qualized		ʃes'cort, *n.*	
e'qualled,		ʃescort', *v.*	
e'qualed		escort'ed	
e'qualling,		ʃespe'cial	
e'qualing		ʃespe'cially	
e'qually		espy'	
equa'tor		*esquire'*	
eq'uerry		es'say	
eques'trian		essayed'	
equilib'rium		es'sayist	
e'quine		es'sence	
equip'		essen'tial	
equip'ment		ʃestab'lish	
equipped'		ʃestab'lished	
eq'uitable		estab'lishing	
eq'uity		estab'lishment	
equiv'alent		estate'	
equiv'ocal		esteem'	
e'ra		esteemed'	
erad'icate		es'timable	
erase'		es'timate, *n.*	
era'ser		es'timate, *v.*	
era'sure		es'timated	
ere		estima'tion	
erect'		estrange'	
erec'tion		estrange'ment	
ergonom'ics		es'tuary	
er'mine		et cet'era, etc.	
erode'		etch	
ero'sion		etch'er	
err		etch'ing	
er'rand		eter'nal	

eter′nity		
e′ther		
ethe′real		
eth′ical		
eth′ics		
eth′yl		
et′iquette		
etymolog′ical		
etymol′ogy		
Euclid		
eu′logy		
euphor′ia		
Europe′an		
evac′uate		
evacua′tion		
evade′		
eval′uate		
evalua′tion		
evan′gelist		
evap′orate		
evap′orated		
evapora′tion		
eva′sion		
eva′sive		
eve		
e′ven		
eve′ning		
e′venly		
e′vensong		
event′		
event′ful		
even′tual		
eventual′ity		
even′tually		
ev′er		
everlast′ing		
everlast′ingly		
ev′ery		
ev′erybody		
ev′erything		
everywhere		
evict′		
evic′tion		
ev′idence		
ev′ident		
ev′idently		
e′vil		

evince′		
evoke′		
evoked′		
evolu′tion		
evolve′		
ewe		
ew′er		
exact′		
exact′ly		
exag′gerate		
exaggera′tion		
exalt′		
exalt′ed		
exalta′tion		
examina′tion		
exam′ine		
exam′iner		
exam′ining		
exam′ple		
exas′perate		
exas′perated		
exaspera′tion		
ex′cavate		
ex′cavated		
excava′tion		
exceed′		
exceed′ingly		
excel′		
excelled′		
ex′cellence		
ex′cellent		
ex′cellently		
excel′sior		
except′		
except′ed		
except′ing		
excep′tion		
excep′tional		
ex′cerpt		
excess′		
excess′ive		
excess′ively		
(exchange′		
(exchanged′		
exchang′ing		
excise′		
excite′		
excite′ment		

exclaim'
exclaimed'
exclama'tion
exclude'
exclu'sion
exclu'sive
exclu'sively
excru'ciate
excur'sion
excu'sable
{excuse', *n.*
{excuse', *v.*
excused'
ex'ecute
ex'ecuted
execu'tion
exec'utive
exec'utor
exec'utrix
exem'plary
exem'plify
exempt'
exemp'tion
ex'ercise
ex'ercised
exert'
exert'ed
exer'tion
exhale'
exhaled'
exha'ling
exhaust'
exhaust'ed
exhaust'ing
exhaus'tion
exhaust'ive
exhaust'ively
exhib'it
exhib'ited
exhib'iting
exhibi'tion
exhibi'tionist
exhib'itor
exhil'arate
exhil'arated
exhilara'tion
exhort'
exhorta'tion

exhort'ed
ex'igency
ex'ile
ex'iled
exist'
exist'ed
exist'ence
exist'ent
existen'tial
exist'ing
ex'it
exor'bitant
expand'
expand'ed
expanse'
expan'sion
expan'sionist
expan'sive
{*expect'*
{*expect'ed*
expect'ant
expect'antly
expecta'tion

expect'ing
expe'diency
expe'dient
expe'diently
ex'pedite
ex'pedited
expedi'tion
expel'
expelled'
expend'
expend'ed
expend'iture
expense'
expen'sive
expen'sively
expe'rience
expe'riencing
exper'iment
experimen'tal
ex'pert
expertise'
expira'tion
expire'
expired'

expi'ry	extinc'tion
explain'	{extin'guish
explained'	{extin'guished
explana'tion	extin'guisher
explan'atory	extol'
explic'it	extolled'
explode'	extor'tion
explo'ded	ex'tra
exploit'	{ex'tract, n.
exploita'tion	{extract', v.
explora'tion	extract'ed
explore'	extrac'tion
explored'	ex'tradite
explor'er	ex'tradited
explo'sion	ex'traditing
explo'sive	extradi'tion
expo'nent	extra'neous
{ex'port, n.	extraor'din-
{export', v.	arily
export'ed	extraor'dinary
export'er	
export'ing	extrav'agance
expose'	extrav'agant
exposi'tion	extrav'agantly
expo'sure	extreme'
express'	extrem'ity
expres'sion	ex'tricate
express'ive	ex'tricated
express'ly	ex'trovert
expul'sion	exu'berance
ex'quisite	exu'berant
ex'tant	exude'
extempora'-	exult'
neous	exulta'tion
extend'	exult'ed
extend'ed	eye
exten'sion	eye'ball
exten'sive	eye'brow
extent'	eyed
exten'uate	
exten'uating	eye'ing, ey'ing
extenua'tion	eye'lash
exte'rior	eye'lid
exter'minate	eye'-op'ener
exter'minated	eyes
extermina'tion	eye'sight
exter'nal	eye'sore
extinct'	eye'wash
	eye'-witness

F

fa'ble
fab'ric
fab'ricate
fabrica'tion
fab'ulous
façade'
face
fac'et
face'tious
face'tiously
fa'cial
fac'ile
facil'itate
facil'itated
facil'ity
facsim'ile
fact
fac'tion
fac'tious
fac'tor
fac'tory
fac'tual
fac'ulty
fad
fad'dist
fade
fade'-out
fag

Fah'renheit   *or*

fail
failed
fail'ing
fail'ure
faint
faint'ed
faintheart'ed
faint'ly
fair
fair'er

fair'est
fair'ly
fair'ness
fair'y
faith
faith'ful
faith'fully
faith'fulness
faith'lessness
fake
faked
fall
falla'cious
fal'lacy
fall'en
fall'ing
fall'-out
false
false'hood
false'ly
falset'to
falsifica'tion
fal'sified
fal'sify
fal'ter
fal'tered
fal'tering
fame
famed
{ famil'iar
{ familiar'ity
familiariza'-
* tion*
famil'iarize
famil'iarized
famil'iarizing
famil'iarly
fam'ily
fam'ine
fam'ish

fam'ished	fatal'ity
fam'ishing	fa'tally
fa'mous	fate
fan	fate'ful
fanat'ic	fa'ther
fanat'ical	fa'ther-in-law
fanat'icism	fa'therland
fan'cied	fa'therless
fan'ciful	fath'om
fan'cifully	fatigue'
fan'cy	fat'ten
fantas'tic	fatu'ity
fantas'tical	fat'uous
fantas'tically	fault
	fault'less
fan'tasy	fault'y
far	fau'na
farce	fa'vour, fa'vor
far'cical	fa'vourable
fare	fa'voured
fared	fa'vourite
farewell'	fa'vouritism
farina'ceous	fawn
farm	fear
farmed	feared
farm'er	fear'ful
farm'house	fear'ing
far'sighted	fear'less
far'ther	feasibil'ity
far'thest	fea'sible
farth'ing	fea'sibly
fas'cinate	feast
fascina'tion	feast'ing
fash'ion	feat
fash'ionable	feath'er
fash'ioned	feath'ery
fast	fea'ture
fast'en	fea'tured
fast'ened	fea'tureless
fast'ener	*Feb'ruary*
fast'er	fed
fast'est	fed'eral
fastid'ious	fed'eralism
fast'ing	fed'eralist
fat	federa'tion
fa'tal	fee
fa'talism	fee'ble
fa'talist	feed

feed'er	
feed'ing	
feel	
feel'ing	
feel'ingly	
feet	
feign	
feint	
felic'itate	
felic'itated	
felicita'tion	
felic'itous	
felic'ity	
fe'line	
fell	
felled	
fel'low	
fel'lowship	
fel'on	
felo'nious	
felo'niously	
fel'ony	
felt	
fe'male	
fem'inine	
fem'inism	
fence	
fenced	
fen'cer	
fend'er	
{fer'ment, *n.*	
{ferment', *v.*	
fermenta'tion	
ferment'ed	
fern	
fero'cious	
feroc'ity	
ferroconc'rete	
fer'ry	
fer'tile	
fertil'ity	
fertiliza'tion	
fer'tilize	
fer'tilizer	
fer'vent	
fer'vently	
fer'vid	

fer'vour, fer'- vor	
fes'ter	
fes'tered	
fes'tival	
fes'tive	
festiv'ity	
fetch	
fetch'ing	
fet'ter	
fet'tered	
feud	
feu'dal	
feuds	
fe'ver	
fe'verish	
fe'verishly	
few	
few'er	
fiancé, fiancée	
fias'co	
fi'at	
fib	
fi'bre	
fi'breglass	
fibrosit'is	
fi'brous	
fick'le	
fic'tion	
ficti'tious	
fid'dle	
fidel'ity	
fidg'et	
fidg'ety	
fidu'ciary	
field	
fiend	
fiend'ish	
fierce	
fierc'est	
fi'ery	
fi'es'ta	
fifteen'	
fifteenth'	
fifth	
fif'ty	
fig	

fight
fight'er
fight'ing
fig'ment
fig'urative
fig'uratively
fig'ure
fig'urehead
figurine'
fil'ament
filch
file
filed
fil'ial
fi'ling
fill
filled
fill'er
fil'let
fil'leted
fill'ing
fill'ip
film
fil'ter
fil'tered
filth
fil'trate
filtra'tion
fin
fi'nal
final'ity
fi'nally
finance'
financed'
{ finan'cial
{ finan'cially
finan'cier
find
find'er
find'ing
fine
fined
fine'drawn
fine'ly
fi'ner
fi'nery
finesse'
fi'nest

fin'ger
fin'gered
fin'ical
fi'nis
fin'ish
fin'ished
fin'ishing
fir
fire
fire'arms
fire'brand
fire'clay
fire'-damp
fired
fire'-engine
fire'man
fire'place
fire'proof
fire'side
fire'wood
fire'works
fir'ing
firm
fir'mament
firm'er
firm'ly
firm'ness
first
first'-class
first'-hand
first'ly
first'-rate
firth
fis'cal
fish
fished
fish'er
fish'ery
fish'-hook
fis'sure
fis'sured
fist
fit
fit'ful
fit'ly
fit'ness

fit'ted	flaunt'ed
fit'ter	fla'vour,
fit'test	fla'vor
fit'ting	fla'voured
fit'tingly	fla'vouring
five	flaw
fiv'er	flaw'less
fix	flax
fixa'tion	flay
fixed	flea
fix'edly	fled
fix'ture	flee
fiz'zle	fleece
fiz'zled	fleet
flab'by	flesh
flac'cid	flew
flag	flexibil'ity
flag'on	flex'ible
fla'grant	flick
fla'grantly	flick'er
flag'-ship	flick'ered
flake	fli'er
flaked	flight
flamboy'ant	flight'y
flame	flim'sily
flan	flim'sy
flange	flinch
flank	fling
flan'nel	flint
flannelette	flip'pancy
flap	flip'pant
flap'per	flip'pantly
flare	flirt
flared	flirt'ing
flash	flit
flashed	flit'ted
flask	flit'ting
flat	float
flat'ly	float'ed
flat'ten	flock
flat'tened	flocked
flat'ter	flog
flat'tered	flogged
flat'terer	flood
flat'tery	flood'ing
flat'ulence	flood'light
flat'ulent	floor
flaunt	floor'ing

flop		flut'tered	
flo'ral		flux	
flor'id		fly	
flor'in		fly'er	
flor'ist		fly'leaf	
floss		fly'over	
flota'tion		fly'-wheel	
flotil'la		foam	
flot'sam		fob	
flounce		fo'cus	
floun'der		fo'cus(s)ed	
floun'dered		fod'der	
flour		foe	
flour'ish		fog	
flour'ished		fogged	
flour'ishing		fog'gy	
flout		foil	
flout'ed		foiled	
flow		foist	
flowed		fold	
flow'er		fold'ed	
flow'ered		fold'er	
flow'ery		fold'ing	
flow'ing		fo'liage	
flown		fo'lio	
fluc'tuate		folk	
fluc'tuated		**folk'lore**	
fluc'tuating		fol'low	
fluctua'tion		fol'lowed	
flue		fol'lower	
flu'ency		fol'lowing	
flu'ent		fol'ly	
flu'ently		foment'	
fluff		fomenta'tion	
fluff'y		fond	
flu'id		fond'er	
fluke		fond'est	
flung		fon'dle	
flunk'ey		fon'dled	
fluores'cent		fond'ly	
flur'ried		food	
flur'ry		food'stuff	
flush		fool	
flushed		fooled	
flus'ter		fool'hardy	
flus'tered		fool'ish	
flute		fool'ishly	
flut'ter		fools'cap	

foot	
foot'ball	
foot'board	
foot'hold	
foot'ing	
foot'lights	
foot'mark	
foot'note	
foot'print	
foot'sore	
foot'step	
foot'stool	
for	
for'age	
for'ay	
forbad', for-	
bade'	
(for'bear, *n.*	
(forbear', *v.*	
forbear'ance	
forbid'	
forbid'den	
force	
forced	
force'ful	
for'ceps	
for'cible	
ford	
ford'ed	
fore	
fore'arm	
forebo'ding	
(fore'cast, *n.*	
(forecast', *v.*	
foreclose'	
foreclo'sure	
fore'court	
fore'father	
forego'	
forego'ing	
foregone'	
fore'ground	
fore'*hand*	
fore'head	
for'eign	
for'eigner	
fore'man	
fore'*most*	

fore'noon	
forerun'ner	
foresee'	
foresee'able	
foreseen'	
foreshad'ow	
fore'sight	
for'est	
forestall'	
forestalled'	
for'ester	
for'estry	
fore*tell'*	
fore'thought	
foretold'	
forev'er	
forewarn'	
forewarned'	
fore'*word*	
for'feit	
for'feited	
for'feiture	
forgave'	
forge	
for'ger	
for'gery	
forget'	
forget'ful	
forget'fulness	
for*give'*	
for*give'*ness	
for*giv'*ing	
forgo'	
forgot'	
forgot'ten	
fork	
forlorn'	
form	
form'al	
formal'ity	
forma'tion	
formed	
for'mer	
for'merly	
for'midable	
for'mula	
for'mulate	
forsake'	

forsa'ken	
forsook'	
fort	
forth	
forth'coming	
forth'right	
forthwith'	
for'tieth	
fortifica'tion	
for'tified	
for'tify	
for'titude	
fort'night	
fort'nightly	
for'tress	
fortu'itous	
for'tunate	
for'tunately	
for'tune	
for'ty	
fo'rum	
for'ward	
for'warded	
for'warding	
for'wards	
fos'sil	
fos'ter	
fos'tered	
fos'tering	
fought	
foul	
fouled	
foul'ly	
found	
founda'tion	
found'ed	
foun'der	
foun'dered	
foun'dry	
fount	
foun'tain	
foun'tain-head	
four	
four'some	
four'teen	
fourteenth'	
fourth	
fowl	

fox	
fracas	
frac'tion	
frac'tious	
frac'ture	
frac'tured	
frag'ile	
fragil'ity	
frag'ment	
frag'mentary	
fra'grance	
fra'grant	
frail	
frail'ty	
frame	
framed	
fra'mer	
frame'work	
franc	
fran'chise	
fran'chisement	
frank	
frank'ly	
frank'ness	
fran'tic	
frater'nal	
frater'nity	
fraud	
fraud'ulent	
fraud'ulently	
fraught	
fray	
frayed	
freak	
freck'le	
free	
freed	
free'dom	
free'hold	
free'lance	
free'ly	
fre'er	
freeze	
freez'ing	
freight	
freight'age	
freight'ed	

French	frivolously
French'man	frock
fren'zied	frog
fren'zy	frol'ic
fre'quency	*from*
fre'quent, adj.	front
frequent', v.	front'age
frequent'ed	fron'tal
frequent'ing	fron'tier
fre'quently	fron'tispiece
fres'co	frost
fresh	frost'bite
fresh'en	frost'ed
fresh'ened	frost'y
fresh'ening	froth
fresh'er	frown
fresh'est	frowned
fresh'ly	frown'ing
fret	froze
fret'ful	fro'zen
fret'ted	fru'gal
fret'ting	frugal'ity
fri'ar	fruit
fric'tion	fruit'ful
Fri'day	fruit'fulness
fried	frui'tion
friend	fruit'less
friend'less	fruit'lessness
friend'lier	frus'trate
friend'liest	frus'trated
friend'liness	frustra'tion
friend'ly	fry
friend'ship	fuch'sia
frieze	fudge
fright	fu'el
fright'en	fu'gitive
fright'ful	fulfil'
fright'fulness	fulfilled'
frig'id	fulfil'ment
frigid'ity	full
frill	full'est
frilled	full'-length
fringe	full'ness
frisk	full'y
frit'ter	ful'some
frit'tered	fum'ble
frivol'ity	fum'bled
friv'olous	fume

fumed		fur'rier	
fu'migate		fur'row	
fu'migated		fur'rowed	
fumiga'tion		fur'ther	
fun		fur'therance	
func'tion		fur'thered	
func'tioned		fur'ther*more*	
fund		fur'ther*most*	
fundamen'tal-		fur'thest	
-ly		fur'tive	
fu'neral		fur'tively	
fune'real		fu'ry	
fun'gus		fuse	
fun'nel		fused	
fun'niest		fu'selage	
fun'ny		fu'sible	
fur		fusillade'	
fu'rious		fu'sion	
fu'riously		fuss	
furl		fuss'y	
furled		fust'y	
fur'long		fu'tile	
fur'lough		futil'ity	
fur'nace		fu'ture	
fur'nish		fu'turist	
fur'nisher		futuris'tic	
fur'niture		futu'rity	

G

gab'erdine
ga'ble
Gael'ic
gadg'et
gaffe
gag
gage
gagged
gai'ety, gay'ety
gai'ly, gay'ly
gain
gained
gain'ing
gait
ga'la
gale
gall
gal'lant, gallant'
gal'lantry
gal'lery
gal'lon
gal'lop
galore'
galvan'ic
gal'vanize
gal'vanized
gam'ble
gam'bler
gam'bling
gam'bol
game
ga'mut
gan'der
gang
gang'ster
gang'way
gaol
gaol'er

gap
gape
garage
garb
gar'bage
gar'den
gar'dener
gar'gle
gar'land
gar'ment
gar'ner
gar'nered
gar'nish
garnishee'
gar'ret
gar'rison
gar'rulous
gar'ter
gas
gash
gashed
gas'-meter
gas'olene
gasom'eter
gasp
gas'tric
gate
gâ'teau
gath'er
gath'ered
gath'ering
gauge
gaunt
gaunt'let
gauze
gave
gay
gay'est
gaze

84

gazed	
gazette'	
gazetteer'	
gear	
geared	
geese	
gel'atine	
gem	
gen'der	
gen'eral	*gen'eral*
general'ity	
generaliza'tion	*generaliza'tion*
gen'eralize	
gen'eralized	
gen'erally	*gen'erally*
gen'erate	
gen'erated	
gen'erating	
genera'tion	
gen'erator	
generosity	
gen'erous	
gen'erously	
gen'esis	
ge'nial	
genial'ity	
ge'nius	
gen'ocide	
genteel'	
Gen'tile	
gen'tle	
gen'tleman	*gen'tleman*
gen'tlemanly	*gen'tlemanly*
gen'tlemen	*gen'tlemen*
gen'tleness	
gen'tly	
gen'uine	
gen'uinely	
geograph'ic	
geograph'ical	
geog'raphy	
geolog'ical	
geol'ogist	
geol'ogy	
geomet'ric	
geomet'rical	
geomet'rically	
geom'etry	

geriat'ric	
germ	
Ger'man	
germane'	
gestic'ulate	
gestic'ulated	
ges'ture	
get	
get'ting	
gey'ser	
ghast'ly	
ghost	
gi'ant	
gibe	
gid'dy	
gift	
gift'ed	
gigan'tic	
gild	
gild'ed	
gill (of a fish)	
gill (a measure)	
gilt	
gimm'ick	
gin	
gin'ger	
gip'sy, gyp'sy	
gird	
gird'ed	
gird'er	
gir'dle	
girl	
girl'hood	
girth	
gist	
give	
giv'en	
giv'er	
gives	
giv'ing	
glacé	
gla'cial	
glac'ier	
glad	
glad'den	
glade	
glad'ly	
glad'ness	

glam'orous
glam'our,
  glam'or
glance
glanced
glan'cing
gland
glare
glared
glass
glass'ful
glass'ware
glass'y
glaze
glazed
gleam
gleamed
glean
gleaned
glee
glen
glib
glide
glim'mer
glimpse
glint
glis'ten
glis'tened
glit'ter
glit'tered
global
globe
gloom
gloom'y
glorifica'tion
glo'rify
glo'rious
glo'ry
gloss
glos'sary
gloss'y
glove
glow
glu'cose
glue
glu'ey
glum
glut

glut'ton
glut'tonous
glyc'erine
gnash
gnaw
gnawed
go
goad
go'-ahead
goal
goat
gob'ble
gob'let
God
god'ly
go'ing
gold
gold'en
gold'smith
golf
golosh'
gone
gong
good
good-bye'
good-
  hu'moured
goodna'ture
goodna'tured
good'ness
good-night'
goods
good'-sized
goodwill'
goose
gore
gored
gorge
gorged
gor'geous
goril'la
gos'pel
gos'sip
got
Goth'ic
gouge

gov'ern	
gov'erned	
gov'erning	
gov'ernment	
governmen'tal	
gov'ernor	or
gov'ernorship	or
gown	
grab	
grace	
grace'ful	
grace'fully	
gra'cious	
gra'ciously	
grada'tion	
grade	
gra'ded	
gra'dient	
gra'ding	
grad'ual	
grad'ually	
grad'uate	
grad'uated	
gradua'tion	
graft	
graft'ed	
graft'er	
graft'ing	
grain	
gram'mar	
gramma'rian	
grammat'ical	
gram'ophone	
gran'ary	
grand	
grand'- daughter	
grand'est	
gran'deur	
grand'father	
grand'mother	
grand'parent	
grand'son	
grange	
gran'ite	
grant	
grant'ed	

gran'ulate	
gran'ulated	
grape	
graph'ic	
graph'ically	
graph'ite	
grap'ple	
grap'pled	
grap'pling	
grasp	
grasped	
grasp'ing	
grass	
grass'y	
grate	
grate'ful	
gratifica'tion	
grat'ified	
grat'ify	
gra'tis	
grat'itude	
gratu'itous	
gratu'ity	
grave	
grav'el	
grave'ly	
gravita'tion	
grav'ity	
gra'vy	
gray, grey	
graze	
grazed	
grease	
greas'y	or
great	
great'er	
great'est	or
great'ly	
great'ness	
Gre'cian	
greed	
greed'ily	
greed'y	
Greek	
green	
green'house	
greet	

greet'ed	grow'er
greet'ing	growl
grega'rious	growled
grew	grown
grey'hound	growth
grid	grub
grief	grudge
griev'ance	grudg'ingly
grieve	grue'some
grieved	gruff
griev'ous	gruff'ly
griev'ously	grum'ble
grill, grille	grum'bled
grilled	grunt
grim	grun'ted
grimace'	guarantee'
grime	guaranteed'
grin	guarantee'ing
grinned	guarantor'
grin'ning	guaranty
grind	*guard*
grind'er	guard'ed
grind'ing	guard'ian
grip	guard'ianship
gripe	*guard'ing*
grit	guess
groan	guessed
groaned	guess'work
groan'ing	guest
gro'cer	guid'ance
gro'cery	guide
groom	guild
groove	guild'hall
grooved	guile
grope	guillotine'
gross	guilt
grotesque'	guilt'y
ground	guin'ea
ground'less	guise
ground'-nut	guitar'
ground'-plan	gulf
ground'work	gull
group	gulled
grouped	gul'let
group'ing	gul'lible
grove	gulp
grov'el	gum
grow	gummed

gump'tion	
gun	
gun'man	
gun'ner	
gun'nery	
gun'powder	
gun'smith	
gun'wale	
gur'gle	
gush	
gushed	
gust	
gust'y	
gut	
gut'ta-per'cha	

gut'ted	
gut'ter	
gut'tural	
guy	
gymna'sium	
gym'nast	
gymnas'tic	
gymnas'tics	
gyrate'	
gyra'ted	
gyra'ting	
gyra'tion	
gy'ratory	
gy'roscope	

H

hab'it
hab'itable
habita'tion
habit'ual
habit'uate
hack
hack'ney
hack'neyed
had
haem'orrhage,
  hem'orrhage
hag
hag'gard
hag'gle
hail
hailed
hair
hair'dresser
hair'y
hale
half
half'-caste
half-heart'ed
half'pence
half'penny
hall
hall'mark
hal'low
halt
halt'ed
hal'ter
halve
halved
ham
ham'hand'ed
ham'let
ham'mer
ham'mered
ham'mock
ham'per

ham'pered
hand
hand'book
hand'ed
hand'ful
hand'icap
hand'icraft
hand'ing
hand'iwork
hand'kerchief
hand'le
hand'led
hand'ling
hand'-made
hand'-out
hand'some
hand'work
hand'writing
hand'y
hang
hang'ar
hanged
hang'er
hang'over
hank'er
haphaz'ard
hap'pen
hap'pened
hap'pening
hap'pier
hap'piest
hap'pily
hap'piness
hap'py
harangue'
harangued'
har'ass
har'bour,
  har'bor

hard	haugh'ty
hard'board	haul
hard'en	haul'age
hard'ened	hauled
hard'er	haunt
hard'est	haunt'ed
hard'-hearted	Havan'a
hard'ly	*have*
hard'ness	ha'ven
hard'ship	*hav'ing*
hard'ware	hav'oc
hard'y	hawk
hare	hawk'er
harm	haw'thorn
harmed	hay
harm'ful	hay'stack
harm'less	haz'ard
harmon'ics	haz'ardous
harmo'nious	haze
har'monize	ha'zel
har'mony	ha'ziness
har'ness	ha'zy
harp	*he*
harpoon'	head
har'row	head'ache
har'rowed	head'light
har'rowing	head'line
harsh	head'long
harsh'ly	headmast'er
har'vest	head'quart'ers
har'vested	
har'vesting	head'strong
has	
hash	head'way
haste	heal
ha'sten	healed
ha'stened	health
ha'stily	health'ful
ha'sty	health'ier
hat	health'iest
hatch	health'y
hatched	heap
hatch'et	hear
hatch'ing	heard
hate	hear'er
hate'ful	hear'ing
hate'fully	hear'say
ha'tred	heart

heart'en	
heart'ening	
heart'felt	
hearth	
heart'ily	
heart'y	
heat	
heat'ed	
heat'er	
heath	
heath'en	
heat'ing	
heave	
heav'en	
heav'enly	
heav'ily	
heav'y	
Hebra'ic	
He'brew	
heck'le	
hec'tic	
hedge	
heed	
heed'ful	
heed'less	
heel	
heif'er	
height	
height'en	
hei'nous	
heir	
heir'ess	
held	
hel'icopter	
hel'iport	
hell	
helm	
helm'et	
help	
help'er	
help'ful	
help'fulness	
help'less	
help'lessness	
hem	
hem'isphere	
hemp	
hemp'en	

hen	
hence	
henceforth'	
hencefor'ward	
her	
her'ald	
her'alded	
her'aldry	
herb	
Hercu'lean	
herd	
herd'ed	
here	
hereaf'ter	
hereby'	
hered'itary	
hered'ity	
herein'	
hereof'	
hereon'	
here*to*'	
heretofore'	
hereun'der	
herewith'	
her'itage	
her'mit	
he'ro	
hero'ic	
he'roin	
her'oine	
her'oism	
her'ring	
hers	
herself'	
hes'itancy	
hes'itant	
hes'itate	
hes'itated	
hes'itating	
hes'itatingly	
hesita'tion	
hew	
hewed	
hewn	
hex'agon	
hia'tus	
hid	

hid'den	hit
hide	hitch
hid'eous	hith'er
hi'ding	hither'to'
hieroglyph'ic	hive
hi'fi	hoard
high	hoard'ed
high'brow	hoard'er
high'er	hoard'ing
high'est	hoarse
high-hand'ed	hoarse'ly
high'land	hoarse'ness
high'ly	hoax
high'ness	hoaxed
high'road	hob'ble
high'way	hob'by
hi'-jacker	hock'ey
hike	hod
hi'ker	hoe
hila'rious	hoed
hilar'ity	hoes
hill	hog
hill'side	hoist
hilt	hoist'ed
him	hoist'ing
himself'	hold
hin'der	hold'er
hin'dered	hold'ing
hin'dering	hold'up
hin'drance	hole
Hin'du	hol'iday
hinge	ho'liness
hint	hol'low
hint'ed	hol'lowed
hint'ing	ho'ly
hip	hom'age
hire	home
hired	home'coming
hire'-pur'chase	home'less
hir'ing	home'ly
his	home'sick
hiss	home'stead
hissed	home'ward
hist'amine	home'work
histo'rian	hom'icide
histor'ic	hom'ily
histor'ical	homoge'neous
his'tory	hom'onym

hon'est	host
hon'estly	hos'tage
hon'esty	hos'tel
hon'ey	host'ess
hon'eymoon	hos'tile
honora'rium	hostil'ity
hon'orary	hot
hon'our,	hotel'
hon'or	hot'house
hon'ourable	hot'ter
hon'oured	hot'test
hon'ours	hound
hood	*hour*
hood'wink	*hour*'ly
hoof	house
hook	house'hold
hop	house'holder
hope	house'keeper
hope'ful	house'keeping
hope'fulness	house'work
hope'less	hous'ing
hope'lessness	hov'el
hop'ing	hov'er
horde	hov'ering
hori'zon	*how*
horizon'tal	*howev'er*
hor'mone	howl
horn	howled
hor'rible	*howsoev'er*
hor'rid	hub
hor'rified	hud'dle
hor'rify	hue
hor'ror	huff
hors-d'oeuv'res	hug
horse	huge
horse'back	hulk
Horse' Guards	hull
horse'hair	hum
horse'man	hu'man
horse'manship	humane'
horse'-power	humane'ly
hort'iculture	humanis'tic
	humanita'rian
hose	human'ity
ho'siery	hu'manly
hos'pitable	hum'ble
hos'pital	hum'bler
hospital'ity	hum'blest

hum'bly	hus'band
hum'bug	hus'banded
hu'mid	hus'banding
humid'ity	hush
humil'iate	hushed
humil'iated	husk
humilia'tion	husk'ily
humil'ity	husk'iness
hummed	husk'y
hu'morist	hus'tle
hu'morous	hus'tled
hu'mour,	hus'tler
hu'mor	hut
hu'moured	hy'brid
hump	hy'drant
hunch	hydraul'ic
hun'dred	hy'drofoil
hun'dredth	hy'drogen
hun'dred-	hy'drophone
weight	hydropon'ics
hung	hy'giene
Hunga'rian	hygien'ic
hun'ger	hymn
hun'gered	hyper'bole
hun'ger-strike	hypercrit'ical
hun'gry	hyperson'ic
hunt	hy'phen
hunt'ed	hypnos'is
hunt'er	hyp'notism
hunt'ing	hyp'notize
hunts'man	hypoc'risy
hur'dle	hyp'ocrite
hurl	hypocrit'ical
hurled	hypothet'ical
hurrah'	hysterec'tomy
hur'ricane	hyste'ria
hur'ried	hyster'ical
hur'ry	hyster'ics
hurt	hythe
hurt'ful	

I

I	
ice	
ice'berg	
ice-cream'	
iced	
i'cicle	
i'cing	
i'cy	
ide'a	
ide'al	
ide'alism	
ide'alist	
idealis'tic	
iden'tical	
iden'tically	
identifica'tion	
iden'tified	
iden'tify	
iden'tity	
id'iocy	
id'iom	
idiomat'ic	
idiosyn'crasy	
id'iot	
idiot'ic	
i'dle	
i'dled	
i'dleness	
i'dol	
i'dolize	
i'dyll	
if	
ignite'	
igni'ted	
igni'tion	
igno'ble	
ignomin'ious	
ignomin'iously	
ig'nominy	
ignora'mus	

ig'norance	
ig'norant	
ig'norantly	
ignore'	
ignored'	
ill	
ill'-bred	
ille'gal	
illegibil'ity	
illeg'ible	
illegi'timate	
illic'it	
illim'itable	
illit'erate	
ill'ness	
illog'ical	
ill'-starred'	
illu'minate	
illu'minated	
illu'minating	
illumina'tion	
illu'mine	
ill'-used	
illu'sion	
illu'sive	
illu'sively	
illu'sory	
ill'ustrate	
ill'ustrated	
illustra'tion	
illus'trative	
illus'trator, ill'ustrater	
illus'trious	
ill-will'	
im'age	
imag'inable	
imag'inary	
imagina'tion	
imag'inative	

imag'ine	im'pact, n.	
imag'ined	impact', v.	
imag'ining	impair'	
im'becile	impaired'	
imbecil'ity	impart'	
imbibe'	impart'ed	
imbibed'	impar'tial	
imbue'	impartial'ity	
imbued'	impas'sable	
im'itate	impas'sioned	
im'itated	impas'sive	
im'itating	impa'tience	
imita'tion	impa'tient	
im'itative	impa'tiently	
im'itator	impeach'	
immac'ulate	impeach'ment	
immate'rial	impecu'nious	
immature'	impede'	
immeas'urable	imped'iment	
imme'diate	impel'	
imme'diately	impelled'	
immemo'rial	impend'	
immense'	impend'ing	
immense'ly	impen'etrable	
immen'sity	impen'itent	
immerse'	imper'ative	
immer'sion	imper'atively	
im'migrant	impercep'tible	
im'migrate	*imper'fect*	
immigra'tion	*imperfec'tion*	
im'minence	*imper'fectly*	
im'minent	impe'rial	
immo'bile	imper'il	
immod'erate	impe'rious	
immod'erately	imper'ishable	
immod'est	imper'sonal	
immod'estly	imper'sonate	
immor'al	impersona'tion	
immoral'ity	imper'tinence	
immor'tal	imper'tinent	
immortal'ity	imper'tinently	
immor'talize	*imperturb'able*	
immov'able	imper'vious	
immune'	impet'uous	
immu'nity	impet'uously	
immu'table	im'petus	
imp	impinge'	
	im'pious	

impla'cable	impress'ively
implant'	(im'print, *n.*
implant'ed	(imprint', *v.*
implement	imprint'ed
im'plicate	impris'on
implica'tion	impris'oned
implic'it	impris'onment
implied'	(im*prob*abil'-
implore'	*ity*
implored'	(im*prob*'able
imply'	(im*prob*'ably
impolite'	impromp'tu
(im'port, *n.*	improp'er
(import', *v.*	improp'erly
(impor'tance	impropri'ety
(impor'tant	(improve'
importa'tion	improved'
import'ed	improve'-
import'er	ment
impor'tunate	improv'idence
importune'	improv'ident
impose'	improv'idently
imposi'tion	*improv'ing*
impossibil'ity	improviza'tion
impos'sible	improvize'
im'post	impru'dence
impos'tor	impru'dent
impos'ture	impru'dently
im'potence	im'pudence
im'potency	im'pudent
im'potent	im'pudently
im'potently	impugn'
impound'	impugned'
impound'ed	im'pulse
impov'erish	impul'sive
impov'erished	impul'sively
impov'erish-	impu'nity
ment	impure'
im*prac*'ticable	impu'rity
impreca'tion	imputa'tion
	impute'
impreg'nable	impu'ted
or	impu'ting
(im'press, *n.*	*in*
(impress', *v.*	inabil'ity
impres'sion	inaccess'ible
impres'sion-	inac'curacy
able	inac'curate
impress'ive	

inac'curately	
inac'tion	
inact'ive	
inactiv'ity	
inad'equacy	
inad'equate	
inadmis'sible	
inadvert'ent	
inadvert'ently	
inane'	
inan'imate	
inani'tion	
inan'ity	
inappro'priate	
inapt'	
inapt'itude	
inartic'ulate	
inartis'tic	
inasmuch'	
inatten'tion	
inatten'tive	
inaud'ible	
inau'gural	
inau'gurate	
inaugura'tion	
inauspi'cious	
inauspi'ciously	
in'born	
in'bred	
incal'culable	
incandes'cence	
incandes'cent	
incapabil'ity	
inca'pable	
incapac'itate	
incapac'itated	
incapac'itating	
incapac'ity	
incar'cerate	
incau'tious	
incau'tiously	
incen'diarism	
incen'diary	
in'cense	
incen'tive	
incep'tion	
inces'sant	

inces'santly	
inch	
in'cidence	
in'cident	
inciden'tal	
incin'erate	
incin'erator	
incip'ient	
inci'sion	
inci'sive	
incite'	
incite'ment	
incivil'ity	
inclem'ency	
inclem'ent	
inclina'tion	
incline'	
inclined'	
inclose'	
inclo'sure	
include'	
inclu'ded	
inclu'ding	
inclu'sion	
inclu'sive	
incoher'ency	
incoher'ent	
in'come	
in'coming	
incom'parable	
incompati- bil'ity	
incompat'ible	
incom'petence	
incom'petent	
incom'petently	
incomplete'	
incomprehen'- sible	
inconceiv'able	
inconclu'sive	
inconclu'sively	
incongru'ity	
incon'gruous	
incon'sequent	
inconsequen'- tial	
inconsid'erable	

inconsid'erate	indeci'sion
inconsist'ency	indeci'sive
inconsist'ent	indeed'
inconspic'- uous	indefat'igable
inconspic'- uously	indefen'sible
	indefin'able
incon'stant	indef'inite
incontest'able	indel'ible
incontrovert'- ible	indel'icacy
	indel'icate
inconve'nience	indem'nify
inconve'- nienced	indem'nity
	indent'
inconve'nient- -ly	indenta'tion
	inden'ture
incor'porate, adj.	{ independ'- ence
incor'porate, v.	{ independ'ent
incor'porated	{ independ'- ently
incor'porating	indescri'bable
incorpora'tion	indeter'minate
incorrect'	in'dex
incorrect'ly	in'dexed
incor'rigible	In'dian
incorrupt'	in'dicate
incorrupt'ible	in'dicated
{ in'crease, n.	indica'tion
{ increase', v.	indic'ative
increased'	in'dicator
increas'ing	ind'ices
increas'ingly	indict'
incred'ible	indict'able
incredu'lity	indict'ment
incred'ulous	{ indif'ference
in'crement	{ indif'ferent
incrim'inate	indif'ferently
incrim'inated	in'digent
in'cubator	indigest'ible
in'culcate	indiges'tion
in'culcated	indig'nant
incum'bent	
incur'	indig'nantly
incur'able	indigna'tion
incur'sion	
indebt'ed	indig'nity
indebt'edness	indirect'
indeci'pherable	indirect'ly

indiscreet'
indiscre'tion
indiscrim'inate
indiscrim'in-
ately
{indispen'-
sable
{indispen'-
sably
indispose'
indisposed'
indisposi'tion
indispu'table
indistinct'
in*distin'guish*-
able
indite'
individ'ual
individ'ualist
individual'ity
individ'ually
indivis'ible
in'dolence
in'dolent
in'dolently
indom'itable
in'door
indorse'
indorse'ment
indors'er
indu'bitable
induce'
induced'
induce'ment
induct'
induc'tion
indulge'
indul'gence
indul'gent
indul'gently
indul'ging
indus'trial
indus'trialist
industrial-
iza'tion
indus'trious
in'dustry
inebria'tion

ined'ible
ineffect'ual
(ineffi'ciency
(ineffi'cient
(ineffi'ciently
inel'egant
inel'igible
inequal'ity

inerad'icable

inert'
iner'tia
ines'timable
inev'itable
inexact'
inexcus'able
inexhaust'ible
inex'orable
inexpe'dient
inexpen'sive
inexpe'rience
inex'plicable
inex'tricable
infallibil'ity
infal'lible
in'famous
in'famy
in'fancy
in'fant
in'fantile
in'fantry
infat'uate
infat'uated
infatua'tion
infect'
infected'
infec'tion
infec'tious
infer'
in'ference
infe'rior
inferior'ity
infer'nal
infer'no
inferred'
infest'
infest'ed
in'fidel

infidel'ity	
in'finite	
in'finitely	
infinites'imal	
infin'ity	
infirm'	
infir'mary	
infir'mity	
inflame'	
inflamed'	
inflammabil'- ity	
inflam'mable	
inflamma'tion	
inflate'	
infla'ted	
infla'ting	
infla'tion	
{inflec'tion	
{inflex'ion	
inflexibil'ity	
inflex'ible	
inflict'	
inflict'ed	
inflic'tion	
in'fluence	
in'fluenced	
in'fluencing	
{*influen'tial*	
{*influen'tially*	
influen'za	
in'flux	
inform'	
inform'al	
informal'ity	
inform'ant	
informa'tion	
inform'ative	
informed'	
inform'er	
inform'ing	
infra'-red	
infre'quent	
infre'quently	
infringe'	
infringe'ment	
infu'riate	

infu'riated	
infuse'	
infused'	
inge'nious	
inge'niously	
ingenu'ity	
ingen'uous	
ingen'uously	
inglo'rious	
in'got	
ingrain'	
in'grate	
ingra'tiate	
ingra'tiated	
ingra'tiating	
ingrat'itude	
ingre'dient	
inhab'it	
inhab'itable	
inhab'itant	
inhab'ited	
inhala'tion	
inhale'	
inhaled'	
inher'ent	
inher'it	
inher'itance	
inher'ited	
inhibi'tion	
inhos'pitable	
inhu'man	
inim'ical	
inim'itable	
iniq'uitous	
iniq'uity	
ini'tial	
ini'tialled, ini'tialed	
ini'tiate	
ini'tiated	
initia'tion	
ini'tiative	
inject'	
inject'ed	
injec'tion	
injudi'cious	
injudi'ciously	
injunc'tion	

in'jure	inscru'table
in'jured	in'sect
inju'rious	insecure'
inju'riously	insecu'rity
in'jury	∫insensibil'ity
injus'tice	⎨insen'sible
ink	⎩insen'sibly
inlaid	insep'arable
in'land	insert'
in'let	insert'ed
in'mate	inser'tion
in'most	∫in'set, *n.*
inn	⎩inset', *v.*
innate'	in'side
in'ner	insid'ious
in'ner*most*	in'sight
in'nocence	insig'nia
in'nocent	insignif'icance
in'nocently	insignif'icant
innoc'uous	insincere'
innova'tion	insincere'ly
innuen'do	insincer'ity
innu'merable	insin'uate
inoc'ulate	insin'uated
inoc'ulated	insin'uating
inocula'tion	insinua'tion
inopportune'	insip'id
inopportune'ly	insist'
inor'dinate	insist'ed
	insist'ence
inorgan'ic	insist'ent
	insist'ently
in'-patient	insobri'ety
in'quest	in'solence
inquire'	in'solent
inquired'	in'solently
inquir'er	insol'uble
inquir'y	insolv'ency
inquis'itive	insolv'ent
inquis'itively	insom'nia
in'road	∫inspect'
insane'	⎨inspect'ed
insan'itary	⎩inspect'ing
insan'ity	inspec'tion
insa'tiable	inspec'tor
∫*inscribe*	inspira'tion
⎨*inscribed'*	inspire'
⎩*inscrib'ing*	inspired'
inscrip'tion	

inspir'ing	
instabil'ity	
install'	
installa'tion	
installed'	
instal'ment	
in'stance	
in'stanced	
in'stant	
instanta'neous	
instanta'ne- ously	
in'stantly	
instead'	
in'step	
in'stigate	
in'stigated	
in'stigator	
instil', instill'	
in'stinct	
instinc'tive	
instinc'tively	
in'stitute	
in'stituted	
institu'tion	
instruct'	
instruct'ed	
instruc'tion	
instruc'tive	
instruct'or	
in'strument	
instrumen'tal	
insubor'dinate	
insubordina'- tion	
insuf'ferable	
(insuffi'ciency	
{insuffi'cient	
(insuffi'ciently	
in'sular	
in'sulate	
in'sulated	
insula'tion	
in'sulator	
in'sulin	
(in'sult, n.	
{insult', v.	
insult'ed	

insult'ing	
insu'perable	
insupport'able	
insur'able	
insur'ance	
insure'	
insured'	
insur'gent	
insurmount'- able	
insurrec'tion	
intact'	
intan'gible	
in'tegral	
in'tegrate	
integ'rity	
in'tellect	
intellec'tual	
intel'ligence	
(intel'ligent	
{intel'ligently	
intel'ligent'sia	
(intel'ligible	
(intel'ligibly	
intem'perance	
intem'perate	
intem'perately	
intend'	
intend'ed	
intense'	
intense'ly	
inten'sify	
inten'sity	
inten'sive	
intent'	
inten'tion	
inten'tional	
intent'ly	
inter	
intercede'	
intercept'	
intercept'ed	
(in'terchange, n.	
{interchange', v.	

interchange'-
able
in'tercom
in'tercourse
interdepend'-
ence
interdepend'-
ent
in'terest
in'terested
in'teresting
interfere'
interfered'
interfer'ence
in'terim
inte'rior
interject'
interjec'tion
interlock'ing
in'terloper

in'terlude

interme'diary
interme'diate

inter'ment
inter'minable
intermin'gle
intermis'sion
intermit'tent
intern'
inter'nal
interna'tional
intern'ment
inter'polate
interpose'
interposed'
inter'pret
interpreta'tion
inter'preted
inter'preter
interred'
inter'rogate
interroga'tion
interrog'atory
interrupt'
interrup'tion
intersect'

intersect'ed
intersec'tion

intersperse'

interspersed'
intertwine'
in'terval
intervene'
interven'tion
in'terview
interwov'en
intes'tate
intes'tine
in'timacy
in'timate, *n.,
adj.*
in'timate, *v.*
in'timately
in'timating
intima'tion
intim'idate
intim'idated
intimida'tion
in'to
intol'erable
intol'erance
intol'erant
intona'tion
intox'icant
intox'icate
intox'icated
intoxica'tion
intrep'id
in'tricacy
in'tricate
intrigue'
intrin'sic
intrin'sically
introduce'
introduced'
introduc'tion
introduc'tory
introspec'tion
introspec'tive
in'trovert
intrude'
intru'ded
intru'sion

intui'tion	invi'ted
intu'itive	invoca'tion
intu'itively	in'voice
in'undate	in'voiced
in'undated	invoke'
inunda'tion	invoked'
inure'	invol'untary
invade'	involve'
in'valid	involved'
inval'id	invul'nerable
inval'idate	*in'*ward
inval'uable	*in'*wardly
inva'riable	i'odine
inva'sion	i'onize
invec'tive	ion'osphere
inveigh'	io'ta
invei'gle	iras'cible
invent'	irate'
invent'ed	ire
inven'tion	I'rish
inven'tive	irk'some
invent'or	
in'ventory	i'ron
inverse'	iron'ic
inver'sion	iron'ical
invert'	*i'*ronmonger
invert'ed	i'rony
invest'	irra'tional
invest'ed	*irrecov'erable*
inves'tigate	*irrecov'erably*
inves'tigated	irredeem'able
investiga'tion	irredu'cible
inves'tigator	irrefu'table
invest'ing	*irreg'ular*
invest'ment	irregular'ity
invest'or	irrel'evancy
invet'erate	irrel'evant
invid'ious	irreme'diable
invigila'tion	*irremov'able*
invig'orate	*irremov'ably*
invig'orated	irrep'arable
invin'cible	irrepres'sible
invi'olable	irreproach'able
invi'olate	irresist'ible
invis'ible	irres'olute
invita'tion	*irrespec'tive*
invite'	*irrespec'tively*

{irrespon- sibil'ity {irrespon'sible	isola'tion
irretriev'able	isola'tionist
irrev'erent	is'otope
irrev'erently	is'sue
irrev'ocable	is'sued
	is'suing
ir'rigate	it
ir'rigated	Ital'ian
irriga'tion	ital'ic
ir'ritable	ital'ics
ir'ritate	ital'icize
ir'ritated	itch
irrita'tion	i'tem
is	i'temize
is'land	itin'erant
is'lander	itin'erary
isle	its
i'solate	itself'
i'solating	i'vory
	i'vy

J

jack			
jack'et			
jack'pot			
Jacobe'an			
jade			
ja'ded			
jag			
jagged			
jag'ged			
jail			
jail'er			
jail'or			
jam			
jamb			
jammed			
jan'gle			
jan'gled			
jan'itor			
Jan'uary			
Japan'			
Japanese'			
jar			
jar'gon			
jar'ring			
jar'ringly			
jaun'dice			
jaunt			
jaun'tily			
jaw			
jay'wa'lker			
jeal'ous			
jeal'ousy			
jeer			
jeered			
jel'ly			
jeop'ardize			
jeop'ardy			
jerk			
jerked			
jer'ry			

jer'sey			
jest			
jest'ed			
jest'er			
jest'ing			
jest'ingly			
jet			
jet'sam			
jet'tison			
jet'ty			
Jew			
jew'el			
jew'eller, jew'eler			
jew'ellery jew'elry			
jew'elry			
Jew'ess			
Jew'ish			
jibe			
jig'saw			
jin'gle			
jitt'ery			
job			
job'ber			
job'bery			
jock'ey			
jocose'			
joc'ular			
jog			
join			
join'er			
join'ing			
joint			
joint'ed			
joint'ly			
joke			
jo'kingly			
jol'lity			
jol'ly			
jolt			

jos'tle		juice	
jos'tled		juke'-box	
jot		July'	
jot'ted		jum'ble	
jot'ting		jum'bo	
jour'nal		jump	
journalese'		jumped	
jour'nalism	*or*	jump'er	
jour'nalist	*or*	junc'tion	
journalis'tic	*or*	junc'ture	
jour'ney		June	
jour'neyed		jun'gle	
jo'vial		ju'nior	
jovial'ity		junk	
joy		*jurisdic'tion*	
joy'ful		ju'rist	
joy'ous		ju'ror	
joy'ously		ju'ry	
ju'bilant		ju'ryman	
jubila'tion		just	
ju'bilee		jus'tice	
judge		jus'tifiable	
judged		*justifica'tion*	
judg'ing		jus'tified	
judg'ment		jus'tify	
ju'dicature		just'ly	
judi'cial		just'ness	
judi'cious		jut	
judi'ciously		jute	
jug		jut'ted	
jug'gle		ju'venile	
jug'gler		juxtaposi'tion	*or*
ju'gular			

K

kangaroo'
keel
keen
keen'er
keen'est
keen'ly
keen'ness
keep
keep'er
keep'ing
keg
ken'nel
kept
kerb
kerb'stone
ker'nel
ker'osene
ket'tle
key
key'board
keyed
key'hole
key'note
kha'ki
kick
kicked
kick'er
kick'ing
kid
kid'nap
kid'napped
kid'napper
kid'ney
kill
kill'joy
kiln
kil'ogramme,
 kil'ogram
kil'ometre,
 kil'ometer

kil'owatt
kilt
kin
kinaesthet'ic
kind
kind'er
kin'dergarten
kind'est
kind'-hearted
kin'dle
kin'dled
kind'ly
kind'ness
kin'dred
king
king'dom
king'-pin
kink
kin'ship
kins'man
kiosk'
kiss
kit
kitch'en
kitchenette'
kite
kith
kit'ten
knack
knap'sack
knave
knead
knee
kneel
kneeled
kneel'ing
knell
knelt
knew
knife

knight		knot'ty	
knight'hood		know	
knit		know'-how	
knit'wear		know'ing	
knives		know'ingly	
knob		*knowl'edge*	
knock		known	
knocked		knuck'le	
knock'er		knuck'led	
knoll		knuck'ling	
knot		ko'dak	
knot'ted		ku'dos	
knot'ting			

L

la'bel
la'belled,
  la'beled
la'belling,
  la'beling
lab'oratory
labo'rious

labo'riously

la'bour, la'bor
la'bourer

labur'num
lab'yrinth
lace
lac'erate
lac'erated
lacera'tion
lach'rymose
la'cing
lack
lackadai'sical

lacked
lacon'ic
lac'quer,
  lack'er
lad
lad'der
la'den
la'dle
la'dy
la'dyship
lag
la'ger
lag'gard
lagged
laid
lain
lair
la'ity

lake
lamb
lam'bent
lame
lamed
lament'
lam'entable

lamenta'tion
lament'ed

lament'ing
lam'inate
lamp
lance
lan'cet
land
land'ed
land'holder
land'ing
land'lady
land'*lord*
land'mark
land'owner
land'-rover
land'scape
land'slide
lane
lan'guage
lan'guid
lan'guish

lan'gour

lank'y
lan'tern
lap
lapel'
lapse
lapsed
laps'ing
lar'ceny

112

larch	launched
lard	launch'ing
lard'er	laun'dry
large	lau'reate
large'ly	lau'rel
larg'er	la'va
larg'est	lav'atory
lark	lav'ender
lar'va	lav'ish
lar'vae	lav'ished
laryngi'tis	lav'ishly
lar'ynx	law
	law'ful
las'car	law'fully
la'ser	law'fulness
lash	law'less
lashed	law'lessness
lash'ing	lawn
lass	law'suit
las'situde	law'yer
last	lax
last'ed	lax'ative
last'ing	lax'ity
last'ingly	lay
last'ly	lay'by
latch	lay'er
late	lay'ing
late'ly	lay'man
la'tent	lay'out
la'ter	laze
lat'eral	la'zier
la'test	la'zily
lath	la'ziness
lathe	la'zy
lath'er	lea
Lat'in	lead (a metal)
lat'itude	lead (to con-
lat'ter	duct)
lat'terly	lead'en
lat'tice	lead'er
laud	lead'ership
laud'able	lead'ing
laud'anum	leaf
laud'atory	leaf'let
laugh	leaf'y
laugh'ingly	league
laugh'ter	leagued
launch	leak

leak'age	le'galize
leak'y	le'gally
lean	legatee'
leaned	lega'tion
lean'est	leg'end
lean'ing	leg'endary
leant	leg'erdemain
leap	legibil'ity
leaped	leg'ible
leap'ing	le'gion
leapt	leg'islate
learn	leg'islated
learned	legisla'tion
learn'ed	*leg'islative*
learn'er	leg'islator
learn'ing	*leg'islature*
learnt	legit'imacy
lease	legit'imate,
lease'hold	*adj.*
lease'holder	legitimate', *v.*
leash	lei'sure
leashed	lei'surely
leas'ing	lem'on
least	lemonade'
leath'er	lend
leave	lend'er
leav'en	lend'ing
lec'ture	length
lec'tured	length'en
lec'turer	length'ening
lec'turing	length'wise
led	length'y
ledge	le'nience
ledg'er	le'niency
leek	le'nient
leer	le'niently
leered	lens
leer'ing	Lent, lent
leer'ingly	leop'ard
lee'ward	lep'er
	lep'rosy
lee'way	les'bian
left	less
left'-handed	lessee'
leg	les'sen
leg'acy	les'sened
le'gal	les'sening
legal'ity	les'ser

les'son	lick
lessor'	licked
lest	lid
let	lid'o
le'thal	lie
lethar'gic	lied
leth'argy	li'en
let'ter	lieu
let'terhead	lieuten'ant
let'terpress	life
let'ting	life'boat
let'tuce	life*guard*
leukaem'ia	life'-insurance
lev'ee	life'less
lev'el	life'-preserver
lev'elled, lev'eled	lifesav'er
lev'elling, lev'eling	life'-size
le'ver	life'time
le'verage	lift
levi'athan	lift'ed
lev'ity	lift'ing
lev'y	lig'ament
liabil'ity	lig'ature
li'able	light
liais'on-officer	light'ed
li'ar	light'ening
li'bel	light'er
li'bellous, li'belous	light'erage
lib'eral	light'hearted
liberal'ity	light'house
lib'erally	light'ing
lib'erate	light'ning
lib'erated	like
lib'erating	like'able
libera'tion	liked
lib'erty	like'lihood
libra'rian	like'ly
li'brary	li'ken
li'cence, *n.*	li'kened
li'cense, *v.*	like'ness
li'censed	like'wise
licensee'	li'lac
licen'tious	lil'y
li'chen	limb
	lim'ber
	lim'bo
	lime

lime'light		liq'uorice,	
lime'stone		lic'orice	
lime'water		lisp	
lim'it		list	
limita'tion		list'ed	
lim'ited		lis'ten	
lim'iting		lis'tened	
lim'ousine		lis'tener	
limp		list'ing	
limped		list'less	
lim'pet		list'lessly	
lim'pid		list'lessness	
limp'ing		lit	
line		lit'any	
lin'eage		lit'eral	
lin'eal		lit'erally	
lineal'ity		lit'erary	
lin'eament		lit'erature	
lin'ear		lithe	
lined		lithog'rapher	
lin'en		lithograph'ic	
li'ner		lithog'raphy	
lin'ger		lit'igant	
lin'gered		lit'igate	
lin'gerie		litiga'tion	
lin'guist		lit'ter	
linguis'tic		lit'tered	
lin'iment		lit'tle	
li'ning		lit'urgy	
link		live, v.	
lino'leum		live, a.	
li'notype		lived	
lin'seed		live'lihood	
lint		live'long	
li'on		live'ly	
li'oness		liv'er	
lip		liv'ery	
lip'stick		lives	
liq'uefy		lives, pl.	
liqueur'		live'stock	
liq'uid		liv'id	
liq'uidate		load	
liq'uidated		load'ed	
liq'uidating		load'ing	
liquida'tion		loaf	
liq'uidator		loaf'er	
liq'uor		loaf'ing	
		loam	

loan		lone'some	
loan'ing		long	
loath, loth		longed	
loathe		long'er, *n.*	
loath'some		lon'ger, *adj.*	
loaves		lon'gest	
lob'by		longev'ity	
lob'ster		long'*hand*	
lo'cal		lon'gitude	
local'ity		longitu'dinal	
lo'calize		long'lived	
lo'cally		long'suffering	
locate'		loo'fah	
loca'ted		look	
loca'ting		looked	
loca'tion		look'ing	
loch		look'out	
lock		loom	
locked		loomed	
lock'er		loom'ing	
lock'et		loop	
lock'out		loop'hole	
lock'smith		loose	
lo'como'tion		loosed	
lo'comotive		loose'ly	
lo'cum-te'nens		loos'en	
lo'cust		loos'ened	
lodge		loos'er	
lodged		loqua'cious	
lodg'ing		loquac'ity	
loft		*lord*	
loft'ier		*lord*'ship	
loft'iest		lore	
loft'ily		lor'ry	
loft'y		lose	
log		los'er	
log'ic		los'ing	
log'ical		loss	
logi'cian		lost	
loin		lot	
loi'ter		lo'tion	
loi'tered		lot'tery	
loll		loud	
lolled		loud'er	
lone		loud'speaker	
lone'liness		lounge	
lone'ly		lov'able	

love
love'lier
love'liest
love'liness
love'ly
lov'er
low
low'er
low'ered
low'est
low'land
low'ly
loy'al
loy'alty
loz'enge
lu'bricant
lu'bricate
lu'bricated
lubrica'tion
lu'bricator
lu'cid
lucid'ity
luck
luck'ier
luck'iest
luck'y
lu'crative
lu'dicrous
lug'gage

luke'warm

lull
lull'aby

lulled
lumba'go
lum'ber
lu'minous
lump
lu'nacy
lu'nar
lu'natic
lunch
lunch'eon
lung
lunge
lurch
lure
lured
lu'rid
lurk
lus'cious
lus'tre
lus'trous
lust'y
lute
luxu'riance
luxu'riant
luxu'rious

luxu'riously

lux'ury
ly'ing
lynch
lynx
lyr'ic
lyr'ical

M

maca'bre
macad'amize
mace
machina'tion
machine'
machin'ery

machine'-tool
machin'ist
mack'erel
mack'intosh
macrobiot'ics
mac'ron
mad
mad'am
mad'den
mad'dening
made
maes'tro
magazine'
mag'ic
mag'ical
magi'cian
magiste'rial
mag'istrate

magnanim'ity

magnan'imous
mag'nate
magne'sia
mag'net
{ *magnet'ic*
mag'netism }
mag'netize
mag'netized
magnet'o
magnif'icence
magnif'icent
magnif'icently
mag'nified

mag'nify
mag'nitude
mahog'any
maid
maid'en
mail
mail'able
mailed
maim
maimed
main
main'land
main'ly
main'spring
main'stay
maintain'
maintain'ed
main'tenance
maize
majes'tic
maj'esty
ma'jor
major'ity
make
ma'ker
make'shift
make'-up
mak'ing
maladjust'ment
mal'ady
mal'aise
mal'aprop
mala'ria
mal'content
male
malev'olent
mal'ice
mali'cious
mali'ciously
malign'

119

malig'nant	man'ly
	mann'equin
maligned'	man'ner
malin'ger	man'nerly
malin'gerer	manoeu'vre
mal'leable	manoeu'vring
mal'nutri'tion	
malt	man'-of-war'
maltreat'	man'or
maltreat'ed	man'power
mama',	man'sion
mamma'	man'slaughter
mam'mal	man'tel
mam'moth	man'telpiece
man	mantil'la
man'acle	man'tle
man'age	man'ual
man'agement	manufac'-
man'ager	ture
man'ageress	manufac'-
manage'rial	tured
man'date, n.	manufac'turer
mandate', v.	manufac'turing
man'datory	manure'
man'dolin	man'uscript
mane	man'y
man'ful	map
man'fully	ma'ple
man'gle	mapped
man'hood	mar
ma'nia	mar'ble
ma'niac	march (March)
mani'acal	marched
man'icure	march'ing
	mare
man'ifest	mar'gin
manifesta'tion	mar'ginal
man'ifested	marine'
man'ifesting	mar'iner
man'ifestly	mar'ital
manifes'to	mar'itime
man'ifold	mark
man'ikin	marked
manip'ulate	mar'ket
manip'ulated	mar'malade
manipula'tion	ma'rocain
mankind'	marred
man'lier	mar'riage

mar'ried	mas'ticated
mar'ring	mastica'tion
mar'row	mas'turbate
mar'ry	masturba'tion
mar'rying	mat
marsh	match
mar'shal	match'ing
mar'shalled,	match'less
mar'shaled	mate
mart	mate'rial
mar'tial	mate'rialist
mar'tyr	materialis'tic
mar'tyrdom	mate'rialize
mar'vel	mater'nal
mar'velled,	mater'nity
mar'veled	mathemat'ic
mar'vellous,	*mathemat -*
mar'velous	*ical*
marx'ist	*mathemat'-*
mascar'a	*ically*
mas'cot	*mathemati'cian*
mas'culine	*mathemat'ics*
mash	mat'inée
mashed	matric'ulate
mask	matric'ulated
mas'ochism	matricula'tion
mas'ochist	matrimo'nial
ma'son	mat'rimony
mason'ic	ma'trix
ma'sonry	ma'tron
masquerade'	ma'tronly
Mass, mass	mat'ter
mas'sacre	mat'ting
	mat'tress
massage'	mature
	matured'
masseur'	matu'rity
masseuse'	maul
mass'ive	mauled
mass'ively	mausole'um
mast	mauve
mas'ter	max'im
mas'tered	max'imize
mas'terful	*max'imum*
mas'tering	may (May)
mas'terly	may'*be*
mas'terpiece	mayonnaise'
mas'tery	may'or
mas'ticate	

may'oral		med'ley	
may'oralty		meek	
may'oress		meek'ly	
maze		meet	
me		meet'ing	
mead'ow		megaloman'ia	
mea'gre		meg'aphone	
meal		meg'aton	
meal'time		mel'ancholy	
mean		mel'low	
mean'est		mel'lowed	
mean'ingless		melo'dious	
meant		melodra'ma	
mean'time		mel'ody	
mean'while		mel'on	
mea'sles		melt	
meas'urable		melt'ed	
meas'ure		melt'ing	
meas'ured		*mem'ber*	
meas'urement		*mem'bership*	
meat		mem'brane	
mechan'ic		memen'to	
mechan'ical		mem'oir	
mechan'-		mem'orable	
ically			
mech'anism		memoran'da	
mechaniza'tion		memoran'dum	
mech'anize		memo'rial	
med'al		mem'orize	
med'dle		mem'orized	
med'dled		mem'orizing	
med'dlesome		mem'ory	
me'dial		men	
me'diate		men'ace	
media'tion		men'aced	
me'diator		men'acing	
med'ical		menag'erie	
medic'inal		mend	
med'icine		menda'cious	
medie'val		mend'ed	
me'diocre		men'dicant	
medioc'rity		mend'ing	
med'itate		me'nial	
med'itated		men'opause	
medita'tion		men'tal	
med'itative		mental'ity	
Mediterra'nean		men'tion	
me'dium		men'tioned	

men'tioning		met'rical	
men'u		metrop'olis	
mer'cantile		*metropol'itan*	
mer'cenary		met'tle	
mer'chandise		Mex'ican	
mer'chant		mias'ma	
mer'ciful		mi'ca	
mer'cifully		mice	
mer'ciless		Mich'aelmas	
mer'cury		mi'crobe	
mer'cy		microb'iol'ogy	
mere		mic'rofilm	
mere'ly		mi'crophone	
merge		mi'croscope	
mer'ger		microscop'ic *or*	
merid'ian		mi'crowave	
meri'no		mid	
mer'it		mid'day	
merito'rious		mid'dle	
mer'riment		mid'dle-aged	
mer'ry		mid'dle-class	
mesh		mid'dleman	
meshed		midg'et	
mes'merize		mid'night	
mes'merized		midst	
mess		mid'summer	
mes'sage		mid'way	
mes'senger		mid'winter	
met		mien	
metab'olism		might	
met'al		might'y	
metal'lic		mi'grant	
metall'urgy		mi'grate	
met'aphor		mi'grated	
metaphor'ical		mil'age	
metapsych'ics		mild	
mete		mild'er	
me'teor		mild'est	
meteor'ic		mil'dew	
me'ter		mild'ly	
meth'ane		mild'ness	
meth'od		mile	
method'ical		mile'age	
Meth'odist		mile'stone	
metic'ulous		mil'ieu	
me'tre		mil'itant	
met'ric		mil'itarism	

militaris'tic	
mil'itary	
mil'itate	
mil'itated	
mili'tia	
milk	
mill	
millen'nium	
mill'er	
mill'ibar	
mill'iner	
mill'inery	
mill'ion	
millionaire'	
mill'stone	
mim'ic	
mince	
mind	
mind'ed	
mind'ful	
mine	
mi'ner	
min'eral	
min'gle	
min'iature	
min'imal	
min'imize	
min'imum	
mi'ning	
min'ion	
min'ister	
min'istered	
ministe'rial	
min'istering	
ministra'tion	
min'istry	
mi'nor	
minor'ity	
min'ster	
min'strel	
mint	
mint'ed	
mi'nus	
minus'cule	
min'ute, *n., v.*	
minute', *adj.*	
minu'tiae	
mir'acle	

mirac'ulous	
mirage'	
mire	
mir'ror	
mirth	
mirth'ful	
mi'ry	
misapplied'	
misapply'	
misapprehend'	
misapprehen'-	
sion	
misappropria'-	
tion	
misbehave'	
misbeha'viour	
miscal'culate	
miscal'culated	
miscalcula'tion	
miscar'ry	
miscella'neous	
miscel'lany	
mischance'	
mis'chief	
mis'chievous	
misconcep'tion	
{miscon'duct, *n.*	
{misconduct', *v.*	
misconstruc'-	
tion	
miscon'strue	
misdeed'	
misdemean'-	
our	
misdirect'	
mi'ser	
mis'erable	
mis'ery	
misfit'	
misfor'tune	
misgiv'ing	
misguide'	
misguid'ed	
mishap'	
{mis*inform'*	
{mis*informed'*	
misinter'pret	

misinterpreta'-
tion
misinter'-
preted
misjudge'
misjudged'
mislaid'
mislead'
misled'
misman'age
misman'aged
misman'age-
ment
misno'mer
misplace'
misprint'
mispronounce'
misquota'tion
misquote'
misquot'ed
mis*represent*'
mis*representa*'-
tion
mis*represent*'ed
mis*represent*'-
ing
misrule'
miss
mis'ses
mis'sile
miss'ing
mis'sion
mis'sionary
miss'ive
mis-spell'
mis'state'ment
mist
mistake'
mista'ken
mistak'enly
mis'took
mis'tress
mistrust'
mistrust'ed
mist'y
mis*under*-
stand'

mis*under*-
stand'ing
mis*understood*'
misuse', *v.*
misuse', *n.*
mite
mit'igate
mit'igated
mitiga'tion
mix
mixed
mix'er
mix'ture
mnemon'ic
moan
mob
mobbed
mo'bile
mobil'ity
mobiliza'tion
mo'bilize
mock
mock'ery
mode
mod'el
mod'elled,
mod'eled
mod'erate,
n., a.
moderate', *v.*
mod'erately
modera'tion
mod'erator
mod'ern
mod'ernist
modernis'tic
moderniza'-
tion
mod'ernize
mod'est
mod'estly
mod'esty
mod'icum
modifica'tion

Moham'medan

Mo'hawk
Mohi'can

moi′ety	mon′ument
moist	{ monumen′-
mois′ten	tal
mois′tened	monumen′-
mois′ture	tally
mo′lar	mood
molas′ses	mood′ily
mold	mood′y
mol′ecule	moon
mole′hill	moon′light
molest′	moon′shine
molesta′tion	moor
molest′ed	moored
molest′ing	moor′land
mol′lify	mop
mol′ten	mope
mo′ment	mo′ped
mo′mentarily	mor′al
mo′mentary	morale′
momen′tous	mor′alist
momen′tum	moral′ity
mon′arch	mor′alize
monar′chical	mor′alizing
mon′archist	mor′ally
mon′astery	morass′
Mon′day	morato′rium
mon′etary	mor′bid
mon′etize	morbid′ity
mon′ey	*more*
mon′key	*moreo′ver*
mon′ogram	mor′ibund
mon′ologue	morn
mon′oplane	morn′ing
monop′olist	moroc′co
monop′olize	morose′
monop′oly	morose′ly
monot′onous	mor′phia
monot′ony	mor′row
monox′ide	mor′sel
monsoon′	mor′tal
mon′ster	mortal′ity
monstros′ity	mor′tar
mon′strous	{ *mort′gage*
mon′tage	{ *mort′gaged*
month	mortgagee′
month′ly	*mort′gaging*
	mort′gagor

mortifica'tion	mourn'fully
mor'tified	
mor'tify	mourn'ing
mor'tuary	mouse
mosa'ic	moustache'
mosqui'to	
moss	mouth
moss'y	mouth'ful
most	mouth'piece
*most'*ly	mov'able,
mote	move'able
motel	move
moth	moved
moth'er	move'ment
mo'ther-craft	mov'er
moth'erhood	mow (to grimace)
moth'er-in-law	(mow (to cut)
mo'tion	(mow (of hay)
mo'tioned	mowed
mo'tionless	mow'er
mot'ivate	*Mr.*
motiva'tion	Mrs.
mo'tive	*much*
mot'ley	mud
mo'tor	mud'dle
mo'tor-bus	mud'dled
mo'tor-car	mud'dy
mo'tor-cy'cle	muf'fle
	muf'fled
mo'torist	muf'ti
mot'orway	mug
mot'tled	mulat'to
mot'to	mul'berry
mould	mulct
mould'ed	mulct'ed
mould'er	mule
mould'ing	multifa'rious
mould'y	mul'tiple
mound	multiplica'tion
mount	multiplic'ity
moun'tain	mult'iplied
mountaineer'	mul'tiply
moun'tainous	mul'titude
mount'ebank	multitu'dinous
mourn	mum'ble
mourn'er	mumps
mourn'ful	munch

mun'dane	mu'tilate
munic'ipal	mu'tilated
municipal'ity	mutila'tion
munif'icence	mu'tiny
munif'icent	mut'ter
munif'icently	mut'tered
muni'tion	mut'tering
mu'ral	mut'ton
mur'der	mu'tual
mur'dered	muz'zle
mur'derer	muz'zled
mur'deress	my
mur'derous	myr'iad
mur'mur	myrrh
mur'mured	myr'tle
mur'muring	*myself'*
mus'cle	myste'rious
mus'cular	myste'riously
muse	mys'tery
mused	mys'tic
muse'um	mys'tical
mush'room	mys'tically
mu'sic	mys'ticism
mu'sical	mystifica'tion
musi'cian	mys'tified
mus'ketry	mys'tify
Muslim	mys'tifying
mus'lin	mystique'
mus'quash	myth
mus'sel	myth'ical
must	myth'ically
mus'tard	mytholog'ic
mus'ter	mytholog'ical-
mus'tered	-ly
mute	mythol'ogy

N

nag		nat'ural	
nail		nat'uralist	
nailed		naturaliza'tion	
nail'ing		nat'uralize	
naïve', naive'		nat'uralized	
na'ked		nat'urally	
name		na'ture	
named		na'turism	
name'less		naught	
name'ly		naugh'ty	
nap		nau'sea	
naph'tha		nau'seate	
nap'kin		nau'tical	
narcot'ic		na'val	
narrate'		nave	
narra'ted		nav'igable	
narra'tion		nav'igate	
nar'rative		nav'igated	
narra'tor		naviga'tion	
nar'row		nav'igator	
nar'rowed		nav'vy	
nar'rower		na'vy	
nar'rowest		nay	
nar'rowing		*near*	
nar'rowly		*near*ed	
nar'row-minded		*near*'er	
na'sal		*near*'est	
nas'ty		*near*'ing	
na'tal		*near*'ly	
na'tion		neat	
na'tional		neat'er	
na'tionalist		neat'est	
national'ity		neat'ly	
nationaliza'-tion		neb'ulous	
na'tionalize		nec'essarily	
na'tionally		nec'essary	
na'tive		neces'sitate	
nativ'ity		neces'sitated	
		neces'sitating	
		neces'sitous	

neces'sity		nes'tle	
neck		nes'tled	
neck'lace		net	
neck'tie		net'ted	
neck'wear		net'ting	
nec'tar		net'tle	
need		net'tled	
need'ed		net'work	
need'ful		neural'gia	
nee'dle		neurasthe'nia	
need'less		neurasthen'ic	
need'lessly		neuri'tis	
need'lessness		neurot'ic	
nee'dlework		neu'ter	
nefa'rious		neu'tral	
nega'tion		neutral'ity	
neg'ative		neu'tralize	
neglect',		neut'ron	
neglect'ed		*nev'er*	
neglect'ful		*nev'ermore*	
neglect'ing		*nevertheless'*	
négligé'		new	
neg'ligence		new'comer	
neg'ligent		new'er	
neg'ligently		new'est	
neg'ligible		newfan'gled	
negotiabil'ity		new-fash'ioned	
nego'tiable		new'ly	
nego'tiate		news	
nego'tiated		news'agent	
negotia'tion		news'paper	
ne'gress		news'print	
ne'gro		*next*	
ne'groid		nib	
neigh		nib'ble	
neigh'bour,		nib'bled	
neigh'bor		nib'bling	
neigh'bour-		nice	
hood		nice'ly	
nei'ther		ni'cest	
Nem'esis		ni'cety	
ne'on		niche	
neph'ew		nick	
Nep'tune		nick'el	
nerve		nick'name	
nerv'ous		nic'otine	
nerv'ously		niece	
nest		nig'gardly	

nigh	
night	
night'gown	
night'ingale	
night'ly	
night'mare	
night'shirt	
night'wear	
nil	
nim'ble	
nine	
nineteen'	
nineteenth'	
nine'tieth	
nine'ty	
ninth	
nip	
nip'ple	
ni'trate	
ni'tric	
ni'trogen	*or*
nitrog'enous	
nit'wit	
no	
nobil'ity	
no'ble	
no'body	
noctur'nal	
nod	
nod'ded	
nod'ding	
nog'gin	
noise	
noise'less	
noise'lessly	
nois'ily	
nois'y	
nom'ad	
nomad'ic	
no'menclature	
nom'inal	
nom'inate	
nomina'tion	
nominee'	
non accep'-tance	

non-appear'-ance	
non-arri'val	
non-attend'-ance	
non'chalance	
non'chalant	
non-com'-batant	
non-commis'-sioned	
non-commit'-tal	
non-*deliv'ery*	
non'descript	
none	
nonen'tity	
non-interven'-tion	
non-par'ty	
nonpay'ment	
non'plussed	
non-res'ident	
non'sense	
nonsen'sical	
non'-stop	
nook	
noon	
noon'day	
nor	
nor'mal	
Nor'man	
north	
north-east'	
north-east'er	
north-east'ern	
north'erly	
north'ern	
north'erner	
north'ward	
north-west'	
north-west'er	
north-west'-erly	
north-west'ern	
Norwe'gian	
nose	

nos'tril	nox'ious
not	noz'zle
notabil'ity	nucleon'ics
no'table	nu'cleus
no'tary	nude
nota'tion	nudge
notch	nu'dism
note	nu'dist
note'book	nug'get
note'worthy	nui'sance
noth'ing	null
no'tice	nul'lified
no'ticeable	nul'lify
no'ticed	nul'lity
no'ticing	numb
not'ifiable	numbed
notifica'tion	*num'ber,*
no'tified	*num'bered*
no'tify	*num'bering*
no'tion	nu'meral
notori'ety	numer'ical
noto'rious	nu'merous
notwithstand'-	nun
ing	nup'tials
nought	nurse
noun	nursed
nour'ish	nurs'ery
nour'ished	nur'ture
nour'ishment	nur'tured
nov'el	nut
nov'elist	nu'triment
nov'elty	nutri'tion
Novem'ber	nutri'tional
nov'ice	nutri'tious
now	nut'shell
now'adays	nyl'on
no'where	nymph
no'wise	

O

O (oh)	
oak	
oar	
oa'sis	
oath	
oat'meal	
oats	
ob'duracy	
ob'durate	
ob'durately	
obe'dience	
obe'dient	
obe'diently	
obese'	
obes'ity	
obey'	
obey'ing	
obit'uary	
ob'ject, n.	
object', v.	
object'ed	
object'ing	
objec'tion	
objec'tionable	
objec'tive	
objec'tively	
obliga'tion	
ob'ligatory	
oblige'	
obliged'	
oblique'	
oblit'erate	
oblit'erated	
oblitera'tion	
obliv'ion	
obliv'ious	
ob'long	
obnox'ious	
obscure'	

obscured'	
obscu'rity	
obse'quious	
observ'ance	
observ'ant	
observa'tion	
observe'	
observed'	
observ'er	
observ'ing	
obsess'	
obsessed'	
obses'sion	
obsoles'cence	
ob'solete	
ob'stacle	
ob'stinacy	
ob'stinate	
obstrep'erous	
obstruct'	
obstruct'ed	
obstruct'ing	
obstruc'tion	
obstruc'tive	
obtain'	
obtain'able	
obtained'	
obtain'ing	
obtrude'	
obtru'ded	
obtru'ding	
obtru'sion	
obtru'sive	
obtru'sively	
obtuse'	
ob'viate	
ob'viated	
ob'viating	
ob'vious	

ob'viously
occa'sion
occa'sional
occa'sioned
occa'sioning
oc'cident
occiden'tal
oc'cupancy
oc'cupant
occupa'tion
oc'cupied
oc'cupier
oc'cupy
oc'cupying
occur'
occurred'
occur'rence
occur'ring
o'cean
o'clock'
oc'tagon
octag'onal
oc'tane
oc'tave
Octo'ber
oc'ulist
odd
o'dious
o'dium
o'dorous
o'dour, o'dor
oes'trogen
oes'trum
of
off
offence'
offend'
offend'ed
offend'er
offend'ing
offen'sive
of'fer
off'hand
of'fice
of'ficer
offi'cial
offi'cially
offi'ciate

offi'ciated
offi'cious
offi'ciously
off'set, n.
offset', v.
off'spring
oft'en
oft'entimes
oh
oil
oil'cloth
oiled
oil'skin
oil'y
oint'ment
old
old'er
old'est
old-fash'ioned
ol'ive
om'elet,
    om'elette
o'men
om'inous
om'inously
omis'sion
omit'
omit'ted
omit'ting
om'nibus
omnip'otence
omnip'otent
omnis'cience
omnis'cient
omniv'orous
on
once
on'cost
one
on'erous
oneself'
one'sided
one'-way
on'ion
on'looker
on'ly
on'set
on'slaught

o'nus		o'ral	
on'ward		or'ange	
on'yx		ora'tion	
ooze		or'ator	
o'pal		or'atory	
opaque'		orb	
o'pen		or'bit	
open-air'		or'chard	
o'pened		or'chestra	
o'pener		orches'tral	
o'pening		or'chestrate	
o'penly		or'chid	
op'era		ordain'	
op'erate		ordained'	
operat'ic			
opera'tion		or'deal	
opera'tional			
op'erative		or'der	
op'erator		or'dered	
operet'ta		or'dering	
opin'ion		or'derliness	
o'pium		or'derly	
oppo'nent		or'dinance	
opportune'		or'dinarily	
opportu'nity		or'dinary	
oppose'		ord'nance	
op'posite		ore	
opposi'tion		or'gan	
oppress'		organ'ic	
oppressed'		organ'ically	
oppres'sion			
oppress'ive		or'ganism	
oppress'ively			
oppress'or		or'ganist	
op'tic		*organiza'tion*	
op'tical		{ *or'ganize*	
opti'cian		{ *or'ganized*	
op'timism		or'ganizer	
op'timist		or'ganizing	
optimis'tic		or'gy	
op'timum		o'rient	
op'tion		orien'tal	
op'tional		or'igin	
op'ulence		orig'inal	
op'ulent		original'ity	
op'us		orig'inate	
or		orig'inated	
or'acle		orig'inating	
		origina'tion	
		orig'inator	

or'nament	outnum'ber-ed
ornamen'tal	outnum'bering
ornamenta'-tion	out-of-date'
ornate'	out-of-doors'
or'phan	out'put
or'thodox	out'rage
	outra'geous
os'cillate	out'right
oscilla'tion	out'set
os'cillograph	out'side
osten'sibly	outsi'der
ostenta'tion	out'size
ostenta'tious	out'skirts
os'teopath	outstand'ing
os'tracize	outstretch'
os'trich	outstrip'
oth'er	outvote'
oth'erwise	out'ward
ought	out'wardly
ounce	out'wards
our	outwit'
ours	o'val
ourselves'	ova'tion
oust	ov'en
oust'ed	*ô'ver*
oust'ing	o'veralls
out	overbal'ance
out'board	overbal'anced
out'break	overbear'ing
out'burst	o'verboard
out'cast	overbur'dened
out'*come*	overcame'
out'cry	o'vercast
out'dated'	{ o'vercharge, n.
outdoors'	{ overcharge', v.
out'er	o'vercoat
out'fit	*overcome'*
out'fitter	overcom'ing
out'going	overcon'fident
out'ing	overcrowd'ed
outland'ish	overdo'
out'law	{ o'verdose, n.
out'lay	{ overdose', v.
out'let	o'verdraft
out'line	overdrawn'
out'look	overdue'
out'lying	

{o'verflow, n.	
{overflow', v.	
overgrown'	
overhang'	
overhaul'	
overhauled'	
over-head'	
o'verheads	
overhear'	
overheard'	
overjoyed'	
o'verland	
{o'verload, n.	
{overload', v.	
overlook'	
o'verpass	
overpow'er	
o'veride'	
overruled'	
overseas'	
oversee'	
o'verseer	
overshad'ow	
o'vershoes	
o'versight	
o'ver-staffed'	
overstep'	
overstrain'	
overtake'	
{o'vertax, n.	
{overtax', v.	
overthrow'	

overthrown'	
o'vertime	
overtook'	
o'verture	
overturn'	
{o'verweight, n.	
{overweight', v.	
overwhelm'	
{o'verwork, n.	
{overwork', v.	
owe	
owed	
owes	
ow'ing	
owl	
own	
owned	
own'er	
own'ership	
own'ing	
ox	
ox'en	
ox'ide	
oxidiza'tion	
ox'idize	
ox'ygen	
oys'ter	
oys'ter-shell	
o'zone	

P

pa
pace
paced
pacif'ic
pac'ified
pa'cifism
pa'cifist
pac'ify
pack
pack'age
pack'er
pack'et
pact
pad
pad'ded
pad'ding
pad'dle
pad'lock
pad'locked
paediat'rics
pa'gan
page
pag'eant
pag'eantry
paid
pail
pain
pained
pain'ful
pain'fully
pain'less
pains
pains'taking
paint
paint'ed
paint'er
paint'ing
pair
pal
pal'ace

pal'atable
pal'ate
pala'tial
pale
pal'ette
palisade'
pall
pal'liate
pallia'tion
pal'liative
pal'lid
pal'lor
palm

palm'ist

pal'mistry

palm'-oil
pal'pable
pal'pitate
pal'pitated
palpita'tion
pal'try
pam'per
pam'pered
pam'pering
pam'phlet
pan
panace'a
panama'
pandemo'nium
pan'der
pan'dered
pane
pan'el
pang
pan'ic
pan'ic-stricken
panora'ma

panoram'ic

138

pant	par′ish
pantech′nicon	parish′ioner
pant′ed	Paris′ian
pan′tomime	par′ity
pan′try	park
papa′	par′king
pa′pal	par′lance
pa′per	par′ley
papy′rus	par′liament
par	*parliamen′tary*
par′able	par′lour
par′achute	par′lous
parade′	paro′chial
par′adise	par′ody
par′adox	parole′
paradox′ical	par′oxysm
par′affin	(parquet′, n.,
par′agon	a.
par′agraph	(par′quet, v.
par′allel	par′ried
par′alleled	par′rot
par′alyse	par′ry
par′alysed	pars′ec
par′alysing	parsimo′nious
	par′simony
paral′ysis	pars′ley
paralyt′ic	pars′nip
par′amount	par′son
paranoi′a	part
par′apet	partake′
parapherna′lia	part′ed
par′aphrase	par′tial
par′asite	partial′ity
pa′rasites	partic′ipant
parasol′	partic′ipate
par′cel	partic′ipated
par′cel(l)ed	partic′ipating
parch	participa′tion
parch′ment	par′ticle
par′don	*partic′ular*
par′donable	partic′ularize
pare	
pa′rent	*partic′ularly*
pa′rentage	part′ing
paren′tal	par′tisan
paren′thesis	parti′tion
parenthet′ic	parti′tioned
parenthet′ical	parti′tionist

part'ly	pa'tron
part'ner	pat'ronage
part'nership	pat'ronize
part'-time	pat'ter
par'ty	pat'tern
pass	pau'city
pass'able	pau'per
pas'sage	pause
passed	paused
pas'senger	paus'ing
pas'sion	pave
pas'sionate	pave'ment
pas'sive	pavil'ion
pas'sively	pav'ing
pass'port	paw
pass*word*	pawn
past	pawn'broker
paste	pawned
paste'board	pawn'shop
pa'sted	pay
pas'tel	pay'able
pastiche'	payee'
pastille'	pay'er
pas'time	pay'ing
past'mas'ter	pay'master
pas'tor	pay'ment
pas'toral	pea
pa'stry	peace
pas'ture	peace'able
pat	peace'ful
patch	peace'fully
pat'ent	peach
pat'ented	peak
patentee'	peal
pater'nal	pealed
path	pear
pathet'ic	pearl
pathet'ically	peas'ant
pa'thos	peas'antry
pa'tience	peb'ble
pa'tient	peck
pa'tiently	pecula'tion
pa'triarch	{*pecu'liar*
pat'riot	{peculiar'ity
patriot'ic	*pecu'liar*ly
pat'riotism	pecu'niary
patrol'	ped'agogic
patrolled'	ped'agogy

ped'al	
ped'ant	
pedan'tic	
ped'dle	
ped'estal	
pedes'trian	
ped'igree	
ped'lar	
peek	
peel	
peeled	
peel'ing	
peep	
peeped	
peep'ing	
peer	
peer'age	
peer'ing	
pee'vish	
pee'vishly	
peg	
pel'let	
pellu'cid	
pelt	
pelt'ed	
pen	
pe'nal	
pe'nalize	
pen'alty	
pen'ance	
pence	
pen'cil	
pen'cil(l)ed	
pend'ant	
pend'ent	
pend'ing	
pen'dulous	
pen'dulum	
pen'etrate	
pen'etrated	
penetra'tion	
penicill'in	
penin'sula	
pe'nis	
pen'itence	
pen'itent	
peniten'tiary	
pen'manship	

pen'niless	
pen'ny	
pen'sion	
pen'sioned	
pen'sioner	
pen'sioning	
pen'sive	
pent	
penu'rious	
pen'ury	
peo'ple	
peo'pled	
pep	
pep'per	
pep'sin	
per	
peram'bulate	
peram'bulator	
per an'num	
perceive'	
per cent'	
percent'age	
percep'tible	
percep'tion	
perch	
per'colate	
per'colator	
percus'sion	
perdi'tion	
per'emptory	
peren'nial	
per'fect	
per'fected	
perfec'tion	
per'fectly	
per'fidy	
per'forate	
perfora'tion	
perform'	
perform'ance	
performed'	
perform'er	
perform'ing	
(per'fume, *n.*	
(perfume', *v.*	
perfunc'tory	

perhaps'		per'sonal	
per'il		personal'ity	
per'ilous		personifica'- tion	
pe'riod		personnel'	
period'ical		*perspec'tive*	
per'iscope		perspicac'ity	
per'ish		perspicu'ity	
per'ishable		perspira'tion	
per'ished		perspire'	
per'jure		persuade'	
per'jurer		persua'ded	
per'jury		persua'sion	
per'manency		persua'sive	
per'manent		pert	
per'manently		pertain'	
per'meate		pertained'	
permis'sible		pertain'ing	
permis'sion		pertinac'ity	
(per'mit, *n.*		per'tinent	
(permit', *v.*		perturb'	
per'mutate		peru'sal	
perni'cious		peruse'	
perox'ide		pervade'	
perpendic'ular		perva'ded	
per'petrate		perverse'	
per'petrated		(per'vert, *n.*	
perpet'ual		(pervert', *v.*	
perpet'uate		pes'simism	
perpet'uated		pes'simist	
perpetu'ity		pessimis'tic	
perplex'		pest	
perplex'ity		pes'ter	
per'quisite		pes'tered	
per'secute		pes'tilence	
persecu'tion		pes'tilent	
per'secutor		pet	
persever'ance		pet'al	
persevere'		peti'tion	
persevered'		peti'tioned	
		peti'tioner	
perseve'ringly		pet'rified	
		pet'rify	
Per'sian		pet'rol	
persist'		petro'leum	
persist'ence		pet'ted	
persist'ent		pet'ticoat	
persist'ently		pet'ty	
persist'ing			
per'son			

pet′ulance	phys′ical
pet′ulant	physi′cian
pew	phys′icist
pew′ter	phys′ics
phan′tasy	physiog′raphy
phan′tom	
pharmaceu′-	physiolog′ical
tical	physiol′ogy
phar′macist	physiothe′rapist
phar′macy	physiothe′rapy
phase	physique′
	pi′anist
phenobar′-	pian′o
bitone	pianofor′te
phenom′ena	piaz′za
	pick
phenom′enal	pick′et
	pick′le
phenom′enon	pic′nic
phi′al	picto′rial
philanthrop′ic	pic′ture
	picturesque′
philan′thropist	pie
	piece
philan′thropy	piece′meal
	piece′-work
philat′elist	pier
philat′ely	pierce
philharmon′ic	pierced
philos′opher	pi′ety
philosoph′ic	pig
philosoph′ical	pig′eon
philos′ophy	pig′eonhole
phlegmat′ic	pig′iron
phob′ia	pig′ment
phonet′ic	pig′my
phonet′ics	pile
phon′ograph	pil′fer
phos′phate	pil′ferage
phos′phide	pil′fered
phos′phorus	pil′ferer
pho′to	pil′fering
pho′tograph	pil′grim
photog′rapher	pil′grimage
photograph′ic	pill
photog′raphy	pil′lage
photogravure′	pil′lar
pho′ton	pil′lion
phrase	
phys′ic	

pil'low	plac'id
pi'lot	pla'giarism
pin	pla'giarize
pin'cers	plague
pinch	plaid
pine	plain
pine'apple	plain'est
pin'ion	plain'ly
pin'ioned	plain'tiff
pink	plain'tive
pin'nacle	plait
pint	plait'ed
pin'-up	plan
pioneer'	plane
pi'ous	plan'et
pi'ously	plank
pip	planned
pipe	plant
pi'per	planta'tion
pi'quancy	plant'ed
pi'quant	plant'er
pique	plas'ter
pi'racy	plas'tered
pi'rate	plas'terer
pis'tol	plas'tic
pis'ton	plate
pit	plateau'
pitch	plat'form
pitch'er	
pit'eous	plat'inum
pit'fall	
pith	plat'itude
pit'iable	plausibil'ity
pit'iful	plau'sible
pit'iless	play
pit'man	played
Pitman'ic	play'er
Pit'manite	play'ful
pit'tance	play'fulness
pit'y	play'ground
piv'ot	play'ing
piv'otal	play'mate
plac'ard, n.	play'room
plac'ard', v.	play'thing
placard'ed	plea
placate'	plead
place	pleas'ant
placed	pleas'antly
	please

pleas'urable		po'etry	
pleas'ure		poign'ancy	
pleat		poign'ant	
plea'ted		point	
plebe'ian		point'ed	
pledge		point'er	
ple'nary		point'ing	
plen'teous		point'less	
plen'tiful		poise	
plen'ty		poi'son	
pli'able		poi'sonous	
pli'ant		poke	
plied		po'lar	
pli'ers		pole	
plight		police'	
plod		police'-court	
plot		police'man	
plough		pol'icy	
ploughed		pol'io	
plough'ing		pol'ish	
pluck		pol'ished	
plug		polite'	
plum		pol'itic	
plu'mage		polit'ical	
plumb		politi'cian	
plumb'er		pol'itics	
plumb'ing		poll	
plumb'-rule		pollute'	
plume		pollu'tion	
plumed		pol'tergeist	
plump		polytech'nic	
plun'der		pol'ythene	
plun'dered		pomp	
plunge		pom'pous	
plu'ral		pond	
plus		pon'der	
plush		pon'dered	
ply		pon'derous	
pneumat'ic		pongee'	
pneumo'nia		pontoon'	
poach		po'ny	
pock'et		pool	
pock'et-book		pooled	
po'em		pool'ing	
po'et		poop	
po'etess		poor	
poet'ic		poor'er	
poet'ical		poor'est	

poor'house	possibil'ity
pop	
pope	pos'sible
pop'lar	post
pop'lin	post'age
pop'pycock	post'al
pop'ulace	post'card
pop'ular	post'date
popular'ity	post'dated
popula'tion	post'er
pop'ulous	poster'ity
porce'lain	post'-free
porch	post-haste'
pore	post'humous
pork	post'ing
por'ous	post'man
por'poise	post'mark
por'ridge	post'master
port	post'-office
port'able	postpone'
port'al	postponed'
portend'	postpone'ment
por'tent	postpon'ing
porten'tous	post'script
port'er	pos'ture
portfo'lio	pot
port'hole	pot'ash
port'ico	potas'sium
port'ière	pota'to
por'tion	pota'toes
portman'teau	po'tency
por'trait	po'tent
por'traiture	poten'tial
portray'	po'tion
portray'al	pot'ter
portrayed'	pot'tery
Portuguese'	pouch
pose	poul'tice
poseur'	poul'try
posi'tion	pounce
pos'itive	pounced
pos'itively	pounc'ing
possess'	pound
possessed'	pour
posses'sion	poured
possess'ive	pov'erty
possess'or	pow'der
	pow'ders

pow'er
pow'erful
pow'erless
*practica*bil'ity
prac'ticable
prac'tical
{ *prac'tice*
{ *prac'tise*
{ *prac'tised*
*prac'tis*ing

practi'tioner   *or*

prai'rie
praise
praised
praise'worthy
prance
pranced
prank
pray
prayed
prayer
pray'ing
preach
preach'er
preach'ing
pream'ble
preca'rious
precau'tion
precau'tionary
precede'
prece'dence
prece'dent, *a.*
prec'edent, *n.*
pre'cept
pre'cinct
pre'cious
prec'ipice
precip'itate,
  n., a.
precip'itate, *v.*
precise'
precise'ly
precis'ion
preclude'
preco'cious
precoc'ity
preconceive'

predeces'sor
predic'ament
predict'
predict'able
predict'ed
predic'tion
predispose'
predom'inance
predom'inant
predom'inantly
predom'inate
pre-em'inence
pre-em'inent
pre'fab
pref'ace
pref'aced
prefer'
pref'erable
pref'erence
preferen'tial   *or*
preferred'
{ pre'fix, *n.*
{ prefix', *v.*
preg'nant
prehistor'ic
{ prej'udice
{ prej'udiced
{ prejudi'cial
{ prejudi'cially
*prej'udic*ing
prel'ate
prelim'inary
prel'ude
premature'
premed'itate
premed'itated
premedita'tion
prem'ier
prem'ise, *n.*
premise', *v.*
pre'mium
pre-nat'al
prepaid'
prepara'tion
prepar'atory

prepare′	
prepared′	
prepar′ing	
prepon′der-	
ance	
prepon′derat-	
ing	
preposi′tion	
prepossess′ing	
prepos′terous	
prereq′uisite	
prerog′ative	or
Presbyte′rian	or
prescribe′	
prescrip′tion	
pres′ence	
{ pres′ent, *n.*, *a.*	
pres′ent′, *v.*	
present′able	
presenta′tion	
pres′ently	
preserva′tion	or
preserv′ative	
preserve′	
preside′	
pres′idency	
pres′ident	
presiden′tial	
presi′ding	
press	
pressed	
press′ing	
pres′sure	
prestige′	or
presu′mably	
presume′	
presumed′	
presump′tion	
presump′tive	
presump′tuous	
pretence′	
pretend′	

pretend′ed	
pretend′ing	
preten′tious	
pre′text	
pret′ty	
prevail′	
prevailed′	
prevail′ing	
prev′alence	
prev′alent	
prevar′icate	
prevar′icator	
prevent′	
prevent′ed	
prevent′ing	
preven′tion	
pre′view	
pre′vious	
pre′viously	
prey	
price	
priced	
price′less	
prick	
prick′ly	
pride	
priest	
pri′marily	
pri′mary	
pri′mate	
prime	
pri′mer	or
prime′val, primae′val	
prim′itive	
prim′rose	
prince	
prin′cess	
{ prin′cipal	
prin′cipally	
prin′cipalship	
prin′ciple	
prin′cipled	
print	
print′ed	
print′er	
print′ing	

pri'or	profan'ity
prior'ity	profess'
pris'on	professed'
pris'oner	profess'ing
pri'vacy	profes'sion
pri'vate	profes'sional
priva'tion	profes'sional-
priv'ilege	ism
prize	profes'sor
probabil'ity	prof'fer
prob'able	prof'fered
prob'ably	*profi'ciency*
pro'bate	*profi'cient*
proba'tion	*profi'ciently*
proba'tionary	pro'file
probe	prof'it
probed	prof'itable
prob'lem	prof'ited
problemat'ic	profiteer'
proce'dure	prof'ligate
proceed'	profound'
pro'cess	profuse'
pro'cessed	profu'sion
proces'sion	prog'eny
proclaim'	proges'terone
proclaimed'	prognos'tic
proclama'tion	prognostica'-
procliv'ity	tion
procon'sul	pro'gramme,
procras'tinate	pro'gram
procrastina'-	pro'gress, *n.*
tion	progress', *v.*
proc'tor	progres'sive
procur'able	prohib'it
procure'	prohib'ited
prod	prohib'iting
prod'igal	prohibi'tion
prodig'ious	prohibi'tive
prod'igy	*pro'ject, n.*
prod'uce, *n.*	*project', v.*
produce', *v.*	*project'ed*
produ'cer	*project'ing*
prod'uct	projec'tion
produc'tion	
produc'tive	project'or
produc'tively	proleta'rian
productiv'ity	proleta'riat
profane'	prolif'erate

prolif'ic		*propor'tionate-*	
pro'logue		*-ly*	
prolong'		propo'sal	
prolonga'tion		propose'	
prolonged'		proposed'	
promenade'		proposi'tion	
prom'inence		propound'	
prom'inent		propound'ed	
prom'inently		propri'etary	
promiscu'ity		propri'etor	
prom'ise		propri'ety	
prom'issory		propul'sion	
promote'		pro ra'ta	
promo'ted		prosa'ic	
promo'ter		prose	
promo'tion		pros'ecute	
prompt		pros'ecuted	
prompt'ed		prosecu'tion	
prompt'ing		pros'ecutor	
prompt'itude		{ pros'pect, *n.*	
prone		{ prospect', *v.*	
pro'noun		prospec'ted	
pronounce'		*prospec'tive*	
pronounce'-		*prospec'tus*	
ment		pros'per	
pronuncia'tion		pros'pered	
proof		prosper'ity	
prop		pros'perous	
propagan'da		{ pros'trate, *a.*	
prop'agate		{ prostrate', *v.*	
propaga'tion		prostra'ted	
propel'		prostra'tion	
propelled'		protect'	
propel'ler		protec'tion	
propen'sity		protec'tionist	
prop'er		**protect'or**	
prop'erly		pro'test, *n.*	
prop'erty		protest', *v.*	
proph'ecy, *n.*		**Pro'testant**	
proph'esied		protesta'tion	
proph'esy, *v.*		protest'ed	
proph'et		protest'ing	
prophet'ic		prot'on	
propi'tiate		protract'	
propi'tiated		protract'ed	
propi'tious		protrude'	
propor'tion-ed		**protrud'ed**	
		proud	

proud'ly	
prove	
proved	
prov'en	
prov'erb	
prover'bial	
provide'	
provi'ded	
prov'idence	
prov'ident	
prov'ince	
provin'cial	
provi'sion	
provi'sional	
provi'so	
provoca'tion	
provoc'ative	
provoke'	
provo'king	
prow'ess	
prowl	
prowled	
proxim'ity	
prox'imo	
pru'dence	
pru'dent	
pruden'tial	
pru'dently	
prune	
Prus'sian	
pry	
psalm	
pseu'do	
pseud'onym	
psychiat'ric	
psychi'atrist	
psychi'atry	
psycho'an'alyst	
psycholog'ical- -ly	
psychol'ogist	
psychol'ogy	
psych'opath	
psychother'apist	
pto'maine	
pub'lic	
pub'lican	

publica'tion	
public'ity	
pub'licly	
{ pub'lish	
{ pub'lished	
pub'lisher	
pub'lishing	
pud'ding	
pud'dle	
pu'erile	
puff	
pu'gilist	
pugna'cious	
pugnac'ity	
puis'ne	
pull	
pulled	
pulp	
pul'pit	
pulsa'tion	
pulse	
pum'ice	
pump	
pumped	
pump'ing	
punch	
punch'-card	
punct'ual	
punctual'ity	
punct'uate	
punct'uated	
punctua'tion	
punct'ure	
pun'ish	
pun'ishment	
pu'nitive	
pu'ny	
pup	
pu'pil	
pup'pet	
pur'chase	
pur'chaser	
pur'chase-tax	
pure	
pure'ly	
purge	
purifica'tion	

pur'ified	
pur'ify	
pur'ity	
purloin'	
pur'ple	
/pur'port, *n.*	
\purport', *v.*	
pur'pose	
pur'poseful	
pur'posely	
purse	
purs'er	
pursu'ant	
pursue'	
pursued'	
pursu'er	

pursuit'	
purvey'	
push	
pushed	
put	
pu'trefied	
pu'trefy	
pu'trid	
put'ter	
put'ting	
put'ty	
puz'zle	
puz'zled	
puz'zling	
pyjam'as	
pyl'on	
pyr'amid	

Q

quack
quacked
quad'rangle
quad'rant
quad'ruped
quad'ruple
quadru'plicate
quaff
quag'mire
quail
quaint
quake
quaked
qua'ker

qualifica'tion

qual'ified
qual'ify
qual'ity
qualm
quan'dary
quan'tify
quan'tity
qua'rantine
quar'rel
quar'reled,
　quar'relled
quar'relsome
quar'ry
quart

quar'ter

quar'terly
quar'termaster
quar'tern
quar'to
quartz
quash
qua'ver
qua'vered

qua'vering
quay
quay'side
queen
queen'ly
queer
quell
quelled
quench
que'ried
quer'ulous
que'ry
quest
ques'tion
ques'tionable
ques'tionably
ques'tioned
ques'tioning
ques'tionnaire
queue
quib'ble
quick
quick'en
quick'ened
quick'er
quick'ly
quick'ness
quick'sand
quick'silver
quick'witted
quies'cent
qui'et
qui'eten
qui'etly
qui'etness
qui'etude
qui'etus
quill
quilt
quinine'

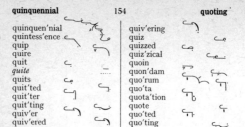

quinquen'nial
quintess'ence
quip
quire
quit
quite
quits
quit'ted
quit'ter
quit'ting
quiv'er
quiv'ered

quiv'ering
quiz
quizzed
quiz'zical
quoin
quon'dam
quo'rum
quo'ta
quota'tion
quote
quo'ted
quo'ting

R

rab'bi		raid
rab'bit		rail
rab'ble		rail'head
rab'id		rail'ing
race		rail'lery
race'course		rail'road
raced		
race'horse		rail'way
ra'cer		rai'ment
ra'cial		rain
ra'cialism		rain'bow
ra'cing		rain'drop
ra'cist		rain'fall
rack		rain'ing
rack'et		rain'proof
ra'dar		rain'-water
ra'diance		rain'y
ra'diant		raise
ra'diate		raised
ra'diated		rai'sin
ra'diating		rake
radia'tion		ral'lied
ra'diator		ral'ly
rad'ical		ral'lying
ra'dii		ram
ra'dio		ram'ble
radioac'tive		ram'bler
ra'diogram		ramifica'tion
radiol'ogist		rammed
rad'ishes		ramp
rad'ium		rampage'
ra'dius		ram'pant
raf'fle		ram'part
raf'fled		ram'shackle
raft		ran
raft'er		ranch
rag		ran'cid
rage		ran'cour,
rag'ged		ran'cor
ra'ging		rand

155

ran'dom	ra'tionalize
rang	rat'tle
range	rau'cous
ran'ger	rav'age
rank	rave
ranked	rav'el
ran'kle	ra'ven
ran'kled	rav'enous
ran'sack	ravine'
ran'som	rav'ish
rant	rav'ished
rap	raw
rapa'cious	ray
rapac'ity	raze
rap'id	ra'zor
rapid'ity	reach
rap'idly	reached
ra'pier	reach'ing
rapped	react'
rap'ping	react'ed
rapt	reac'tion
rap'ture	reac'tionary
rap'turous	reac'tor
rare	read
rare'ly	read, *p.t.*
rar'ity	read'able
ras'cal	readdress'
rascal'ity	read'er
rash	read'ier
rash'ly	read'ily
rasp	read'iness
rasp'berry	read'ing
rat	readjust'
rat'able	readjust'ed
rate	readjust'ment
rate'able	readmis'sion
rate'payer	readmit'
rate'payers	read'y
rath'er	read'ymade
ratifica'tion	reaffirm'
rat'ified	re'al
rat'ify	re'alism
ra'ting	re'alist
ra'tio	realist'ic
ra'tion	real'ity
ra'tional	re'alizable
rationaliza'-tion	realiza'tion
	re'alize

re'alized	recant'
re'alizing	recapit'ulate
re'ally	recapitula'tion
realm	recap'ture
ream	recast'
rean'imate	recede'
reap	rece'ded
reaped	rece'ding
reap'er	receipt'
reap'ing	receiv'able
reappear'	receive'
reappear'ance	received'
reappoint'	receiv'er
reappoint'ment	receiv'ership
reappor'tion	re'cent
rear	re'cently
reared	recep'tacle
re-arrange'	recep'tion
re-arrange'ment	recep'tionist
rea'son	recep'tive
rea'sonable	receptiv'ity
rea'sonably	recess'
rea'soned	reces'sion
reassem'ble	reces'sional
reassert'	re'charge'
reassu'rance	rec'ipe
reassure'	recip'ient
re'bate, n.	recip'rocal
rebate', v.	recip'rocate
reb'el, n.	reciproca'tion
rebel', v.	reciproc'ity
rebelled'	reci'tal
rebell'ion	recita'tion
rebell'ious	recite'
rebound'	reci'ted
rebuff'	reci'ting
rebuild'	reck'less
rebuild'ing	reck'lessness
rebuilt'	reck'on
rebuke'	reck'oned
rebut'	reck'oning
rebut'tal	reclaim'
rebut'ting	reclaimed'
recal'citrant	reclama'tion
recall'	recline'
recalled'	reclined'
recall'ing	recli'ning
	recluse'

recogni'tion	rectan'gular
recog'nizance *or*	rec'tify
rec'ognize	rec'tifying
ruc'ognized	rec'titude
recoil'	rec'tor
recoiled'	recum'bent
recollect'	recu'perate
recollec'tion	recu'perated
recommend'	recu'perating
recommenda'tion	recupera'tion
rec'ompense	recu'perative
rec'oncile	recur'
rec'onciled	recurred'
reconcilia'tion	recur'rence
recondi'tion	recur'rent
reconnoi'tre	recur'ring
reconsid'er	red
reconsidera'tion	redeem'
reconsid'ered	redeem'able
reconsid'ering	redeemed'
reconstruct'	redemp'tion
reconstruct'ed	redeploy'
reconstruct'ing	red'-hot
reconstruc'tion	redistrib'ute
rec'ord, *n.*	red'olent
record', *v.*	redoub'le
record'er	redound'
recount'	redound'ed
recount'ed	redress'
recount'ing	red'-tape'
recoup'	reduce'
recourse'	reduced'
recov'er	redu'cing
recov'erable	reduc'tion
recov'ered	redun'dant
recov'ery	re-ech'o
rec'reant	re-ech'oed
rec'reate	reed
recrea'tion	reef
recrim'inate	reef'er
recrimina'tion	reek
recruit'	reel
recruit'ed	re-elect'
recruit'ment	re-elect'ed
rect'angle	re'-elec'tion
	reeled
	re-embark'
	re-enact'

re-enact'ment

re-enforce'

re-engage'

re-en'ter

re-en'tered

re-*estab'lish*
re-*estab'-
  lished*
re-*estab'lish-
  ment*

re'-examina'-
  tion

re-exam'ine

referee'

refer'

ref'erence

referen'dum

referred'

refer'ring   *or*

refill'

refine'

refine'ment

refi'ner

refi'nery

refit'

reflect'

reflect'ed

reflec'tion

reflec'tive

reflect'or

re'flex, *n., adj.*

reflex', *v.*

reform'

reforma'tion   *or*

reform'atory

reformed'
reform'er
reform'ing

refrac'tion

refrac'tory

refrain'

refrained'

refresh'

refreshed'

refresh'ing

refresh'ment

refrig'erate

refrig'erated

refrig'erating

refrigera'tion

refrig'erator

ref'uge

refugee'

refund'

refund'ed

refund'ing

refu'sal

ref'use, *n., a.*
  refuse', *v.*

refuta'tion

refute'

refu'ted

refu'ting

regain'

regained'

re'gal

regale'

regaled'

rega'lia

re'gally

regard'

regard'ed

regard'ing

regard'less

re'gency

regen'erate, *n.,
  adj.*

regen'erate, *v.*

regen'erated

regenera'tion   *or*

re'gent

régime'

reg'imen

reg'iment

regimen'tal

re'gion

re'gional

reg'ister

reg'istered

reg'istering

reg'istrar   *or*

registra'tion

reg'istry

regret'		reit'erate	
regret'ful		reit'erated	
regret'table		reitera'tion	
regret'ted		reject'	
regret'ting		reject'ed	
reg'ular		rejec'tion	
regular'ity		rejoice'	
reg'ularly		rejoiced'	
reg'ulate		rejoin'	
reg'ulated		rejoin'der	
reg'ulating		rejoined'	
regula'tion		relapse'	
reg'ulator		relapsed'	
rehabil'itate		relate'	
rehabilita'tion		rela'ted	
rehears'al		rela'tion	
rehearse'		rela'tionship	
rehearsed'		rel'ative	
rehears'ing		rel'atively	
reign		relativ'ity	
reigned		relax'	
reimburse'		relax'ation	
reimbursed'		relaxed'	
reimburse'-		relay', *n.*	
ment		re-lay', *v.*	
rein		release'	
reincarna'tion		released'	
rein'deer		releas'ing	
reined		rel'egate	
reinforce'		relega'tion	
reinforced'		relent'	
reinforce'ment		relent'ed	
reinforc'ing		relent'ing	
		relent'less	
reinsert'		rel'evancy	
reinsert'ed		rel'evant	
re*inspec'tion*		reliabil'ity	
reinstate'		reli'able	
reinstat'ed		reli'ance	
reinstate'ment		reli'ant	
reinstat'ing		rel'ic	
re*insur'ance*		relied'	
reinsure'		relief'	
reinvest'		relieve'	
re*invest'ment*		relieved'	
reis'sue			
reis'sued		relig'ion	or

relig'ious	*or*
relig'iously	*or*
{ relin'quish	
{ relin'quished	
relin'quishing	
rel'ish	
rel'ished	
reluc'tance	
reluc'tant	
reluc'tantly	
rely'	
rely'ing	
remain'	
remain'der	
remained'	
remain'ing	
remand'	
remand'ed	
remark'	
{ remark'able	
{ remark'ably	
remarked'	
remark'ing	
reme'dial	
rem'edy	
{ remem'ber	
{ remem'bered	
remem'bering	
remem'brance	
remind'	
remind'ed	
remind'er	
remind'ing	
reminis'cence	
reminis'cent	
remiss'	
remis'sion	
remit'	
remit'tance	
rem'nant	
remod'el	
remon'strance	
remon'strant	
remon'strate	
remon'strated	
remon'strating	

remorse'	
remorse'ful	
remorse'less	
remote'	
remote'ly	
remov'able	
remov'al	
remove'	
removed'	
remov'ing	
remu'nerate	
remu'nerated	
remunera'tion	
remu'nerative	
rend	
ren'der	
ren'dered	
ren'dering	
ren'dezvous	
ren'egade	
renew'	
renew'al	
renewed'	
renew'ing	
renounce'	
renounced'	
ren'ovate	
renova'tion	
renown'	
renowned'	
rent	
rent'al	
rent'ed	
renum'ber-ed	
renuncia'tion	
reoc'cupy	
reop'en	
reorganiza'tion	
{ reor'ganize	
{ reor'ganized	
reor'ganizing	
reorienta'tion	
repaid'	
repair'	
repaired'	
repair'er	
repair'ing	
repara'tion	

repartee'		reprehen'sion	
repass'		*represent'*	
repast'		*representa'tion*	
repay'		*represent'ative*	
repay'able		*represent'ed*	
repay'ment		*represent'ing*	
repeal'		repress'	
repealed'		repressed'	
repeat'		repres'sion	
repeat'edly		reprieve'	
repeat'ing		reprieved'	
repel'		repriev'ing	
repelled'		(rep'rimand, *n.*	
repel'lent		(reprimand', *v.*	
repent'		(re'print, *n.*	
repent'ance		(reprint', *v.*	
repent'ant		reprint'ed	
repent'ed		repri'sal	
repent'ing		reproach'	
repercus'sion		reproached'	
repertoire'		reproach'ful	
rep'ertory		reproach'fully	
repeti'tion		reproach'ing	
repeti'tious		rep'robate	
repet'itive		reproduce'	
repine'		re*produc'tion*	
repined'		re*produc'tive*	
repi'ning		reproof'	
replace'		reprove'	
replace'able		reproved'	
replace'ment		rep'tile	
replen'ish		*repub'lic*	
replen'ished		*repub'lican*	
replen'ishing		re*publica'tion*	
replete'		(repub'lish	
reple'tion		(repub'lished	
rep'lica		repu'diate	
replied'		repu'diated	
reply'		repu'diating	
reply'ing		repudia'tion	
report'		repug'nance	
report'ed		repug'nant *or*	
report'er			
report'ing		repulse' *or*	
repose'		repulsed'	
repos'itory		repuls'ing	
reprehend'		repul'sion	
reprehensible			

repul'sive		res'idency	
repul'sively		res'ident	
rep'utable		residen'tial	
reputa'tion		resid'ual	
repute'		resid'uary	
repu'ted		res'idue	
request'		resign'	
request'ed		resigna'tion	*or*
request'ing	*or*	resigned'	
req'uiem		resign'ing	
require'		resil'ience	
required'		resil'iency	
require'ment		resil'ient	
requir'ing		res'in	
req'uisite		resist'	
requisi'tion		resist'ance	
requisi'tioned		resist'ed	
requisi'tioning		res'olute	
requi'tal		res'olutely	
requite'		resolu'tion	
re-read		resolve'	
re-read', *p.t.*		resolved'	
rescind'		resolv'ing	
rescind'ed		res'onance	
res'cue		res'onant	
res'cued		resort'	
res'cuer		resort'ed	
res'cuing		resound'	
research'		resound'ed	
resem'blance		resource'ful	
resem'ble		resource	
resem'bled		*respect'*	
resent'		*respect*abil'ity	
resent'ed		*respect'*able	
resent'ful		*respect'*ably	
resent'ing		*respect'ed*	
resent'ment		*respect'*ful	
reserva'tion		*respect'*fully	
reserve'		*respect'*ing	
reserved'		*respect'*ive	
reserv'ing		*respect'*ively	
res'ervoir		respira'tion	
reset'		res'pirator	
reship'ment		respir'atory	
reside'		res'pite	
resi'ded		resplen'dent	
res'idence			

respond'
respond'ed
respon'der
respond'ing
response'
responsibil'-
  ities
{responsibil'-
  ity
{respon'sible
respon'sive
rest
res'taurant
restau'rateur
rest'ed
rest'ful
rest'fully
rest'fulness
rest'ing
restitu'tion
rest'ive
rest'less
rest'lessly
rest'lessness
restora'tion
restor'ative
restore'
restored'
restrain'
restrained'
restrain'ing
restraint'
restrict'
restrict'ed
restrict'ing
restric'tion
result'
result'ant
result'ed
resume'
résumé'
resumed'
resu'ming
resump'tion
resurrec'tion
resus'citate

resuscita'tion
re'tail, n., a.
retail', v.
retail'er
retain'
retained'
retal'iate
retal'iated
retal'iating
retalia'tion
retard'
retard'ed
reten'tion
reten'tive
ret'icence
ret'icent
ret'ina
ret'inue
retire'
retired'
retire'ment
retir'ing
retort'
retort'ed
retouch'
retrace'
retraced'
retra'cing
retract'
retreat'
retreat'ed
retreat'ing
retrench'
retrench'ment
retribu'tion
retrieve'
retrieved'
retriev'er
retriev'ing
ret'rograde
ret'rograded
ret'rospect
retrospec'tion
retrospec'tive
retrospec'tively
return'
return'able
returned'

return'ing		revolt'	
reu'nion		revolt'ed	
reunite'		revolt'ing	
revalua'tion		revolu'tion	
reveal'		revolu'tionary	
revealed'		revolu'tionize	
reveal'ing		revolve'	
rev'el		revolved'	
revela'tion		revolv'er	
rev'elry		revul'sion	
revenge'		reward'	
revenged'		reward'ed	
revenge'ful		reward'ing	
rev'enue		rewrite'	
rever'berate		rewrit'ten	
rever'berated		rhap'sody	
rever'berating		rhe'ostat	
reverbera'tion		rhes'us	
reverb'erator		rhet'oric	
revere'		rhetor'ical	
revered'		rheumat'ic	
rev'erence		rheum'atism	
rev'erend		rheu'matoid	
rev'erent		rhinoc'eros	
rev'erie		rhu'barb	
revers'al		rhyme	
reverse'		rhythm	
reversed'		rhyth'mic	
revers'ible		rhyth'mical	
revert'		rib	
revert'ed		rib'ald	
revert'ing		rib'bon	
review'		rice	
reviewed'		rich	
review'er		rich'er	
review'ing		rich'es	
revile'		rich'est	
revise'		rich'ly	
revised'		rid	
revi'sing		rid'dance	
revi'sion		rid'dle	
revi'sionary		ride	
revi'sionist		ri'der	
revis'it		ridge	
revi'val		rid'icule	
revive'		rid'iculed	
revived'		ridic'ulous	
revoke'			

ridic'ulously		ri'pened	
rid'ing		ri'pening	
rife		ripped	
riff'raff		rip'ping	
ri'fle		rip'ple	
ri'fled		rise	
ri'fling		ris'en	
rift		risibil'ity	
rig		ris'ible	
right		ri'sing	
right'-angle		risk	
right'-angled		risked	
right'eous		risk'ing	
right'eousness		risk'y	
right'ful		ris'qué	
right'fulness		rite	
right'-*hand*		rit'ual	
right'ing		ri'val	
right'ly		ri'val(l)ed	
rig'id		ri'val(l)ing	
rigid'ity		ri'valry	
rig'or		riv'er	
rig'orous		riv'et	
rig'our		riv'eted	
rile		riv'eting	
riled		road	
ri'ling		road'hog	
rim		road'side	
rime		road'ster	
rind		road'way	
ring		road'worthy	
ringed		roam	
ring'er		roamed	
ring'ing		roam'er	
ring'leader		roan	
ring'let		roar	
ring'-road		roared	
rink		roast	
rinse		roast'ed	
rinsed		roast'er	
rins'ing		roast'ing	
ri'ot		rob	
ri'oter		rob'ber	
ri'otous		rob'bery	
ri'otously		robe	
rip		rob'in	
ripe		rob'ot	
ri'pen		robust'	

robust'ly	rotate'
rock	rota'ted
rock'er	rota'tion
rock'ery	rote
rock'et	rot'ted
rock'ing	rot'ten
rod	rot'ting
rode	rotund'
ro'dent	rotund'ity
rode'o	rou'ble
roe	rouge
rogue	rough
rogu'ish	rough'en
rogu'ishly	rough'er
rôle	rough'ly
roll	round
rolled	round'about
roll'er	round'ed
roll'ing	round'ing
roll'ing-stock	round'ly
ro'man,	rouse
Ro'man	roused
romance'	rous'ing
roman'tic	rout
romp	route
romped	routine'
romp'ing	rove
rood	ro'ver
roof	ro'ving
roof'ing	row (a rank)
roof'less	row (a tumult)
room	row'diness
room'y	row'dy
roost	row'dyism
roost'er	rowed
root	row'lock
root'ed	roy'al
rope	roy'alist
ro'sary	roy'ally
rose	roy'alty
ro'seate	rub
ros'in	rubbed
ros'ter	rub'ber
ros'trum	rub'bing
ro'sy	rub'bish
rot	ru'by
Rota'rian	ruc'tion
ro'tary	rudder

rude		run	
rude'ness		run'away	
ru'diment		run'-down'	
rudimen'tal		run'way	
rudimen'tary		rung	
rue		run'ner	
rued		run'ning	
rue'ful		rupee'	
rue'fully		rup'ture	
ruf'fian		rup'tured	
ruf'fle		ru'ral	
ruf'fled		ruse	
ruf'fling		rush	
rug		rushed	
rug'ged		rush'ing	
ru'in		rusk	
ruina'tion		rus'set	
ru'ined		Rus'sian	
ru'ining		rust	
ru'inous		rus'tic	
rule		rus'ticate	
ruled		rust'ing	
ru'ler		rus'tle	
ru'ling		rus'tled	
rum		rus'tling	
rumble		rust'y	
ru'minate		rut	
rum'mage		ruth	
ru'mour,		ruth'less	
ru'mor		ruth'lessly	
rump		ruth'lessness	
rum'ple		rye	
rum'pled			

S

Sab'bath	
sa'ble	
sabotage'	or
sa'bre	
sack	
sack'ing	
sac'rament	
sa'cred	
sac'rifice	
sac'rificed	
sac'rilege	
sacrile'gious	
sad	
sad'den	
sad'der	
sad'dest	
sad'dle	
sad'dled	
sad'dler	
sa'dism	
sad'ly	
safa'ri	
safe	
safe-con'duct	
safe'-depos'it	
safe'guard	
saf'er	
saf'est	
safe'ty	
saga'cious	
sagac'ity	
sage	
said	
sail	
sailed	
sail'ing	
sail'or	
saint	
saint'ly	
sake	

sal'ad	
sal'aried	
sal'ary	
sale	
sale'able	
sales'man	
sales'manship	
sales'woman	
sa'lient	
salin'ity	
sal'low	
sall'y	
salm'on	
saloon'	
salt	
salt'ed	
salt'ing	
salu'brious	
sal'utary	
saluta'tion	
salute'	
salu'ted	
sal'vage	
salva'tion	
salve	
salved	
Samar'itan	
same	
sam'ple	
sanato'rium	
sanc'tified	
sanc'tify	
sanc'tion	
sanc'tioned	
sanc'tioning	
sanc'tity	
sanc'tuary	
sanc'tum	
sand	
san'dal	

sand'stone		saun'tered	
sand'wich		saun'tering	
sand'y		sau'sage	
sane		sav'age	
sang		sav'agely	
san'guine		save	
san'itary		sa'viour	or
sanita'tion		sa'vour,	
san'ity		sa'vor	
sank		sa'voury	
sap		savoy'	
sap'per		saw	
sap'phire		saw'dust	
sar'casm		sawed	
sarcas'tic		saw'ing	
sarcas'tically		saw'mill	
sardine'		sawn	
sa'ri		saw'yer	
sarong'		Sax'on	
sarsaparil'la		sax'ophone	
sartor'ially		say	
sash		say'ing	
sat		says	
satch'el		scab'bard	
sate		scaf'fold	
sa'ted		scaf'folding	
sateen'		scald	
sa'tiate		scale	
sa'tiated		scaled	
sati'ety		scalp	
sat'in		scamped	
sat'ire		scam'per	
satir'ical		scam'pered	
sat'irist		scam'pering	
satisfac'tion		scam'pi	
satisfac'torily		scan	
satisfac'tory		scan'dal	
sat'isfied		scan'dalous	
sat'isfy		scan'ner	
sat'urate		scant	
sat'urated		scant'ily	
sat'urating		scant'ly	
satura'tion		scant'y	
Sat'urday		scar	
sauce		scarce	
sauce'pan		scarce'ly	
sau'cer		scarce'ness	
saun'ter		scar'city	

scare
scare'monger
scarf
sca'ring
scar'let
scarred
scathe
sca'thing
scat'ter
scat'tered
scat'tering
scenar'io
scene
sce'nery
sce'nic
scent
scent'ed
scep'tic,
  skep'tic
scep'tical
scep'ticism
scep'tre
sched'ule
  or (U.S)
sched'uled
scheme
sche'mer
schizophren'ia
schnör'kel
schol'ar
schol'arly
schol'arship
scholas'tic
school
school'boy
schooled
school'fellow
school'girl
school'house
school'master
school'mistress
school'room
school'teacher
schoon'er
sciat'ica
sci'ence
scientif'ic
scientif'ically

sci'entist
scin'tillating
scis'sors
scoff
scoffed
scoff'er
scoff'ing
scold
scone
scoop
scoot'er
scope
scorch
score
scored
scor'er
scor'ing
scorn
scorn'ful   *or*
scorn'fully   *or*
scorn'ing
Scot
Scotch, scotch
Scots'man
Scot'tish
scoun'drel
scour
scourge
scout
scowl
scowled
scowl'ing
scram'ble
scram'bled
scram'bling
scrap
scrape
scratch
scrawl
scrawled
scream
screamed
screech
screen
screened
screw

screwed	
scrib'ble	
scrib'bled	
scrim'mage	
scrip	
script	
Scrip'ture	*or*
scroll	
scrounge	
scrub	
scrubbed	
scru'ple	
scru'pulous	
scru'pulously	
scru'pulous-ness	
scru'tinize	
scru'tiny	
scuf'fle	
scuf'fled	
scull	
scull'er	
scull'ery	
sculp'tor	
sculp'ture	
scum	
scur'ried	
scur'rilous	
scur'ry	
scut'tle	
scythe	
sea	
sea'board	
sea'borne	
sea'-coast	
sea'faring	
seal	
sealed	
sea'-level	
seal'skin	
seam	
sea'man	
sea'manship	
seamed	
sea'plane	
sea'port	
search	

search'er	
search'ing	
search'light	
sea'shore	
sea'side	
sea'son	
sea'sonable	
sea'sonal	
sea'soned	
seat	
seat'ed	
seat'ing	
sea'ward	
sea'weed	
sea'worthy	
secede'	
seclude'	
seclu'sion	
seclu'sive	
Sec'onal	
sec'ond	
sec'ondary	
sec'onded	
sec'onder	
sec'ond-*hand*	
sec'ondly	
sec'ond-rate	
sec'onds	
se'crecy	
se'cret	
secreta'rial	
secreta'riat	
sec'retary	
secrete'	
secre'ted	
secre'tion	
se'cretive	
sect	
secta'rian	
sec'tion	
sec'tional	
sec'tionalize	
sec'tor	
sec'ular	
secure'	
secured'	
secure'ly	
secu'ring	

secu'rity
sedate'
sed'entary
sed'iment
sedi'tion
sedi'tious
see
seed
see'ing
seek
seem
seemed
seem'ingly
seen
seethe
seeth'ing
seg'ment
seg'regate
segrega'tion
segrega'tionist
seismol'ogy
seize
seized
seiz'ing
sei'zure
sel'dom
select'
select'ed
select'ing
selec'tion
select'ive
select'or
self
self-addressed'
self'-assur'ance
self-con'fidence
self-con'scious
self-contained'
self-control'
self-defence'
self-determina'-
  tion
self-esteem'
self-ev'ident
self-explan'-
  atory
self in'terest
self'ish

self'ishly
self'ishness
self-possessed'
self-posses'sion
self-reli'ance
self-*respect*'
self-*service*'
self-willed'
sell
sell'er
Sel'lotape
selves'
sem'aphore
sem'blance
sem'ibreve
sem'icircle
sem'icolon
sem'inar
sem'inary
sen'ate
sen'ator
send
send'er
send'ing
se'nile
senil'ity
se'nior
senior'ity
sensa'tion
sensa'tional
sense
sense'less
sense'lessly
sense'lessness
sensibil'ity
sen'sible
sen'sibly
sen'sitive
sen'sitively
sen'sitiveness
sen'sual
sent
sen'tence
sen'tenced
sen'tient
sen'timent
sentimen'tal-ly
sen'tinel

sen'try	seventeenth'
sep'arate, *adj.*	sev'enth
sep'arate, *v.*	sev'entieth
sep'arated	sev'enty
sep'arating	sev'er
separa'tion	{sev'eral
sep'arator	{sev'erally
Septem'ber	sev'erance
sep'tic	severe'
sepul'chral	sev'ered
sep'ulchre	severe'ly
se'quel	sev'ering
se'quence	sever'ity
seques'tered	sew
serenade'	sew'age
serene'	sewed
serene'ly	sew'er
seren'ity	sew'erage
serge	sew'ing
ser'geant	sewn
se'rial	sex
seria'tim	sex'ton
se'ries	sex'y
se'rious	shab'by
se'riously	shack
se'riousness	shack'le
ser'jeant	shack'led
ser'mon	shade
serv'ant	shad'ow
serve	shad'owy
served	sha'dy
serv'ice	shaft
serv'iceable	shaft'ing
serv'ile	shake
servil'ity	sha'ken
serv'ing	sha'ker
serv'itude	sha'ky
ses'sion	*shall*
set	shal'low
set'back	shal'lower
set'ting	sham
set'tle	shame
set'tled	shamed
set'tlement	shame'ful
set'tler	shame'fully
set'tling	shame'less
sev'en	shampoo'
seventeen	shampooed'

shampoo'ing	
sham'rock	
shape	
shape'less	
share	
shared	
share'holder	
sha'ring	
shark	
sharp	
sharp'en	
shar'pened	
shar'pening	
sharp'er	
sharp'est	
sharp'ly	
shat'ter	
shat'tered	
shave	
shaved	
shav'ing	
shawl	
she	
sheaf	
shear	
sheared	
shear'ing	
shears	
sheath	
sheathe	
sheaves	
shed	
sheen	
sheep	
sheep'ish	
sheep'ishly	
sheer	
sheet	
sheet'ing	
shelf	
shell	
shellac'	
shell'ac	
shelled	
shell'fish	
shel'ter	
shel'tered	
shel'tering	

shelve	
shemoz'zle	
shep'herd	
sher'bet	
sher'iff	
sher'ry	
shield	
shield'ed	
shield'ing	
shift	
shift'ed	
shift'ing	
shift'less	
shift'y	
shil'ling	
shim'mer	
shim'mered	
shim'mering	
shin	
shine	
shin'gle	
shi'ning	
shi'ny	
ship	
ship'builder	*or*
ship'building	
ship'ment	
ship'owner	
ship'per	
ship'ping	
ship'yard	
shire	
shirk	
shirked	
shirk'er	
shirk'ing	
shirt	
shiv'er	
shiv'ered	
shiv'ering	
shoal	
shock	
shod	
shod'dy	
shoe	
shoe'maker	
shone	

shook		
shoot		
shoot'ing		
shop		
shop'keeper		
shop'ping		
shop'-stew'ard		
shore		
shorn		
short		
short'age		
short'bread		
short'-circ'uit		
short'coming		
short'en		
short'er		
short'est		
short'hand		
short'ly		
shorts		
short'sighted		
short'-term		
shot		
should		
shoul'der		
shout		
shout'ed		
shout'ing		
shove		
shov'el		
shov'el(l)ed		
show		
show'down		
showed		
show'er		
show'ered		
show'ering		
show'ing		
show'manship		
shown		
show'room		
show'y		
shrank		
shrap'nel		
shred		
shrewd		
shriek		
shrill		

shrine		
shrink		
shrink'age		
shrink'ing		
shriv'el		
shroud		
shroud'ed		
shrub		
shrug		
shrunk		
shrunk'en		
shud'der		
shud'dered		
shuf'fle		
shuf'fled		
shun		
shunt		
shunt'ed		
shunt'ing		
shut		
shut'ter		
shut'tle		
shy		
shy'ly		
sick		
sick'en		
sick'le		
side		
side'board		
side'-car		
side'-effect		
side'light		
si'ding		
si'dle		
siege		
sieve		
sift		
sift'ed		
sigh		
sighed		
sigh'ing		
sight		
sight'seeing		
sight'seer		
sign		
sig'nal		
sig'natory		
sig'nature		

sign'board		sin'ewy	
signed		sin'ful	
sign'er		sin'fully	
signif'icance		sing	
signif'icant		singe	
signif'icantly		singed	
significa'tion		singe'ing	
{sig'nified		sing'er	
{sig'nify		sing'ing	
sig'nifying		sin'gle	
sign'ing		sin'gle-handed	
sign'post		sin'gular	
sign'*writ'er*		singular'ity	
si'lence		sin'ister	
si'lencer		sink	
si'lent		sin'ner	
si'lently		sip	
silhouette'		si'phon	
silicos'is		sip'ping	
silk		sir	
sil'ly		sire	
sil'ver		si'ren	
sil'verware		sir'loin	
sim'ilar		sis'al	or
similar'ity		sis'ter	
sim'ilarly		sis'ter-in-law	
sim'ile		sit	
simil'itude		site	
sim'mer		sit'ter	
sim'mered		sit'ting	
sim'mering		sit'uate	
sim'per		sit'uated	
sim'pered		situa'tion	
sim'ple		six	
sim'pler		six'pence	
simplic'ity		six'penny	
simplifica'tion		sixteen'	
sim'plify		sixteenth'	
sim'ulate		sixth	
sim'ulated		six'ty	
simulta'neous		size	
sin		size'able	
since		skate	
sincere'		ska'ted	
sincere'ly		ska'ter	
sincer'ity		ska'ting	
si'necure		skel'eton	
sin'ew		sketch	

sketched		
sketch'ily		
sketch'ing		
sketch'y		
skew		
skew'er		
ski	or	
skid		
skid'ding		
skiff		
skil'ful		
skill		
skilled		
skim		
skimmed		
skimp		
skin		
skinned		
skin'ning		
skip		
skipped		
skip'per		
skir'mish		
skir'mished		
skirt		
skull		
sky		
sky'lark		
sky'light		
sky'scraper		
sky'way		
slab		
slack		
slack'en		
slack'ened		
slag		
slain		
sla'lom		
slam		
slan'der		
slan'dered		
slan'dering		
slan'derous		
slang		
slant		
slant'ed		
slant'ing		
slap		

slapped		
slap'ping		
slash		
slashed		
slash'ing		
slate		
slaugh'ter		
slaugh'tered		
slaugh'ter-house		
slave		
sla'very		
sla'vish		
sla'vishly		
slay		
slay'er		
sledge		
sleek		
sleep		
sleep'er		
sleep'ily		
sleep'ing		
sleep'less		
sleep'lessness		
sleep'y		
sleet		
sleeve		
sleigh		
sleight		
slen'der		
slept		
sleuth		
slew		
slice		
sliced		
slick		
slid		
slide		
slide'-rule		
sli'ding		
slight		
slight'est		
slight'ly		
slim		
slime		
sling		
slink		
slip		

slip′per	smat′tering
slip′pery	smear
slip′ping	smeared
slip′road	smear′ing
slip′shod	smell
slit	smelled
slo′gan	smelt
slope	smelt′ed
slot	smelt′er
sloth	smile
sloth′ful	smiled
slot′ted	smi′lingly
slouch	smith
slough (a bog)	smog
slough (a cast skin)	smoke
slov′enly	smo′ker
slow	smooth
slow′ly	smooth′er
slow′ness	smote
slug	smoth′er
slug′gard	smoth′ered
slug′gish	smoul′der
slug′gishly	smoul′dered
sluice	smudge
slum	smug′gle
slum′ber	smug′gled
slum′bered	smug′gler
slum′bering	snack′-bar
slump	snag
slung	snail
slur	snake
slurred	snap
slur′ring	snapped
slush	snap′shot
sly	snare
smack	snared
small	sna′ring
small′er	snarl
small′est	snarled
smart	snatch
smart′en	snatched
smart′er	snatch′ing
smart′est	sneak
smart′ly	sneer
smash	sneered
smashed	sneer′ing
smat′ter	sneeze
	sniff

sniv'el		soiled	
snob		soj'ourn	
snob'bery		sol'ace	
snob'bish		so'lar	
snoop		sold	
snoop'er		sol'der	
snore		sol'dered	
snort		sol'dier	
snow		sole	
snow'drift		sole'ly	
snowed		sol'emn	
snow'fall		solem'nity	
snow'shoes		solemniza'tion	
snow'storm		sol'emnize	
snub		sol'emnly	
snuff		solic'it	
snug		solicita'tion	
so		solic'ited	
soak		solic'itor	
soaked		solic'itous	
soap		solic'itude	
soar		sol'id	
soared		solidar'ity	
sob		solid'ified	
so'ber		solid'ify	
sobri'ety		solid'ity	
so'-called		sol'idly	
socc'er			
sociabil'ity		solil'oquize	
so'ciable		solil'oquized	
so'cial		solil'oquy	
so'cialism		sol'itary	
so'cialist		sol'itude	
socialist'ic		so'lo	
soci'ety		so'loist	
sociol'ogy		solubil'ity	
sociom'etry		sol'uble	
sock		solu'tion	
sock'et		solve	
sod		solved	
so'da		solv'ency	
so'fa		solv'ent	
soft		som'bre	
sof'ten		some	
sof'tener		some'body	
soft'ly		some'*how*	
soft'wood		some'one	
soil		som'ersault	

some'thing		soured	
some'time		south	
some'what		south-east'	
some'where		south-east'ern	
son		south'erly	
song		*south'ern*	
song'ster		south'erner	
son'ic		south'ward	
son'-in-law		south-west'	
son'net		south-west'ern	
sonor'ity		souvenir'	
sono'rous		sov'ereign	
sono'rously		sov'ereignty	
soon		Sov'iet	
soon'er		sow (pig)	
soot		sow (to scatter)	
soothe		sowed	
soothed		sow'er	
sooth'ing		sow'ing	
sop		sown	
sophis'ticated		space	
sophistica'tion		spaced	
soporif'ic		space'-man	
sopra'no		space'-ship	
sor'did		space'-station	
sor'didness		space'-suit	
sore		spa'cious	
sor'row		spa'ciously	
sor'rowful		spade	
sor'rowfully		span	
sor'rowing		span'gle	
sor'ry		Span'iard	
sort		span'iel	
sort'ed		Span'ish	
sort'er		spanned	
sort'ing		spar	
sought		spare	
soul		spared	
sound		spar'ing	
sound'ed		spar'ingly	
sound'er		spark	
sound'est		spark'le	
sound'ing		spark'led	
sound'proof		spark'ling	
sound'track		spar'row	
soup		sparse	
sour		sparse'ly	
source		spar'city	

Spar'tan	spell'bound
spasm	spelled
spasmod'ic	spell'ing
spasmod'ically	spelt
spat	spend
spate	spend'ing
spat'ter	spend'thrift
speak	spent
speak'er	sphere
speak'ing	spher'ical
spear	sphinx
spe'cial	spice
spe'cialist	spi'der
special'ity	spike
specializa'tion	spill
spec'ialize	spilled
spe'cially	spilt
spec'ialty	spin
spe'cie	spin'ach
spe'cies	spi'nal
specif'ic	spin'dle
specif'ically	spine
specifica'tion	spin'ster
spec'ified	spi'ral
spec'ify	spire
spec'ifying	*spir'it*
spec'imen	spir'ited
spe'cious	*spir'it*ual
speck	spit
spec'tacle	spite
spectac'ular	spite'ful
specta'tor	spite'fulness
spec'tre	splash
spectrom'eter	splashed
spec'ulate	splash'ing
spec'ulated	spleen
spec'ulating	splen'did
specula'tion	splen'didly
spec'ulative	splen'dour
spec'ulator	splice
sped	splint
speech	splin'ter
speed	splin'tered
speed'ily	splin'tering
speedom'eter	split
speed'way	splutter'
speed'y	splut'tered
spell	splut'tering

spoil	spur
spoiled	spu'rious
spoilt	spurn
spoke	spurned
spo'ken	spurn'ing
spokes'man	spurred
sponge	spurt
spon'sor	spy
spon'sored	spy'ing
spontane'ity	squab'ble
sponta'neous	squad
spool	squad'ron
spoon	squal'id
sporad'ic	squall
sport	squall'y
sport'ing	squal'or
sports'man	squan'der
sports'manship	squan'dered
sports'wear	squan'dering
spot	square
spot'-check	squash
spot'less	squaw
spouse	squeak
spout	squeal
sprain	squeam'ish
sprained	squeeze
sprain'ing	squint
sprang	squire
sprawl	squirm
sprawled	squir'rel
sprawl'ing	squirt
spray	stab
spread	stabbed
spread'ing	stabil'ity
sprig	sta'bilize
spright'ly	sta'bilizer
spring	sta'ble
spring'ing	stack
spring'time	sta'dium
sprin'kle	staff
sprin'kled	stag
sprint	stage
sprout	stage'craft
sprout'ed	stag'ger
spruce	stag'gered
sprung	stag'gering
spry	stag'nant
spun	stagna'tion

staid		start'ling	
stain		starva'tion	
stained		starve	
stain'less		starved	
stair		starv'ing	
stair'case		state	
stair'way		sta'ted	
stake		state'less	
staked		state'ly	
stale		state'ment	
stalk		state'room	
stalked		states'man	
stalk'er		states'manlike	
stall		states'manship	
stal'wart		stat'ic	
stam'ina		stat'ically	
stam'mer		sta'ting	
stam'mered		sta'tion	
stam'mering		sta'tionary	
stamp		sta'tioned	
stamped		sta'tioner	
stampede'		sta'tionery	
stanch		statis'tical	
stand		statis'tically	
stand'ard		statisti'cian	
standardiza'-tion		statis'tics	
stand'ardize		stat'ue	
stand'-by'		stat'ure	
stand'-*in*		sta'tus	
stand'ing		stat'ute	
stand'point		stat'utory	
stand'still		staunch	
sta'ple		stave	
star		stay	
starch		stayed	
starch'iness		stay'ing	
stare		stead	
stared		stead'fast, sted'fast	
sta'ring		stead'fastly	
stark		stead'ied	
star'ring		stead'ier	
star'ry		stead'iest	
start		stead'ily	
start'ed		stead'y	
start'er		steak	
start'le		steal	
start'led		stealth	

stealth'y	stew'ardess
steam	stew'ardship
steam'boat	stich, stick
steamed	stiff
steam'er	stiff'en
steam'roller	stiff'ened
steam'ship	sti'fle
steed	sti'fled
steel	sti'fling
steel'yard	stig'ma
steep	stig'matize
stee'ple	still
steer	stim'ulant
steer'age	stim'ulate
steered	stim'ulated
steer'ing	stim'ulating
stem	stimula'tion
stench	stim'ulus
sten'cil	sting
stenog'rapher	stint
stenograph'ic	stint'ed
stenog'raphy	stint'ing
	sti'pend
sten'otypist	stip'ulate
stento'rian	stip'ulated
step	stip'ulating
step'-ladder	stip'ulation
stepped	stir
step'ping	stirred
step'ping-stone	stir'ring
	stir'rup
ster'eotyped	stitch
ster'ile	stitched
steril'ity	stitch'ing
steriliza'tion	stock
ster'ilize	stock'broker
ste'rilizer	stock'holder
ster'ling	stock'ing
stern	stock'ist
stern'er	stock'pile
stern'est	stock'piling
stern'ly	
stet	stock'taking
steth'oscope	stodg'y
ste'vedore	stoic
stew	sto'ical
stew'ard	sto'icism
	stoke

stok'er		strait'en	
stok'ing		strait'ened	
stole		strand	
sto'len		strand'ed	
stol'id		strange	
stom'ach		strange'ly	
stone		*stran'ger*	
stood		stran'gle	
stooge		stran'glehold	
stool		strap	
stoop		straphang'er	
stop		stra'ta *or*	
stop'page		strat'agem	
stop'ping		strateg'ic	
stor'age		strat'egy	
store		strat'osphere	
stored		stra'tum *or*	
store'keeper		straw	
stor'ing		straw'berry	
storm		straw'board	
stor'y		stray	
stout		strayed	
stout'er		streak	
stout'est		stream	
stout'heart'ed		streamed	
stout'ly		stream'ing	
stove		stream'line	
stow		street	
stow'age		strength	
stow'away		strength'en	
stowed		strength'ened	
stow'ing		strength'ening *or*	
strad'dle		stren'uous	
strag'gler		stren'uously	
straight		streptococ'cus	
straight'away		streptomy'cin	
straight'en		stress	
straight'ened		stretch	
straight'ening		stretch'er	
straight'er		stretch'ing	
straight'est		strew	
straightfor'- ward		strewed	
strain		strick'en	
strained		strict	
strain'er		strict'er	
strain'ing		strict'est	
strait		strict'ly	
		stric'ture	

stride		stud'ying	
stri'dent		stuff	
strife		stum'ble	
strike		stum'bled	
stri'ker		stum'bling	
stri'king		stum'bling- block	*or*
string		stump	
strin'gency		stumped	
strin'gent		stun	
strip		stunned	
stripe		stung	
strip'tease		stunt	
strive		stunt'ed	
strode		stupefac'tion	
stroke		stu'pefy	
stroll		stupen'dous	
strolled		stu'pid	
strong		stupid'ity	
stron'ger		stu'pidly	
stron'gest	*or*	stu'por	
strong'hold		stur'dy	
strong'ly		stut'ter	
strong'minded		stut'tered	
strong'room		stut'tering	
strop		style	
strove		styled	
struck		styl'i	
struc'tural		sty'lish	
struc'ture		sty'lishly	
strug'gle		sty'lo	
strug'gled		suave	*or*
strug'gling		subal'tern	
strung		subaquat'ic	
strut		subcommit'- tee	
strut'ted		subdivide'	
strych'nin, strych'nine		subdivi'sion	
stub'born		subdue'	
stub'bornness		subdued'	
stuc'co		subed'it	
stuck		sub'hu'man	
stud		(sub'ject, a.	
stud'ded		{subject', v.	
stu'dent		(subject'ed, p.p.	
stud'ied		subject'ing	
stu'dio		subjec'tion	
stu'dious		subjec'tive	
stud'y			

subjectively 188 sufferer

subjec'tively		substantia'- tion	
subjoin'		sub'stitute	
subjoined'		sub'stituted	
sublet'		substitu'tion	
sublime'		subsume'	
sublim'ity		sub'terfuge	
sub'marine		subterra'nean	
submerge'		sub'tle	
submers'ible		sub'tlety	
submis'sion		subtract'	
submiss'ive		subtract'ed	
submit'		subtrac'tion	
submit'ted		sub'urb	
submit'ting		subur'ban	
subnor'mal		suburb'ia	
subor'dinate, n., a.		sub'urbs	
		sub'way	
subor'dinate, v.		succeed'	
subordina'tion		succeed'ed	
		succeed'ing	
subpoe'na	or	success'	
subscribe'		success'ful	
subscribed'		success'fully	
subscri'ber		succes'sion	
subscrib'ing		succes'sive	
subscrip'tion		succes'sively	
sub'sequent		success'or	
sub'sequently		succinct'	
subserv'ient		suc'cour, suc'cor	
subside'		succumb'	
subsi'ded		succumbed'	
subsi'dence		such	
subsid'iary		suck	
sub'sidize		suck'le	
sub'sidized		suc'tion	
sub'sidizing		sud'den	
sub'sidy		sud'denly	
subsist'		sud'denness	
subsist'ed		sue	
subsist'ence		sued	
subson'ic		suède	
sub'stance		su'et	
substan'tial		suf'fer	
substan'- tially		suf'ferance	
substan'tiate		suf'fered	
substan'tiated		suf'ferer	

suffice'	
sufficed'	
suffi'ciency	
suffi'cient	
suffi'ciently	
suf'fix, *n.*	
suffix', *v.*	
suf'focate	
suf'focated	
suf'focating	
suffoca'tion	
suf'frage	
sug'ar	
suggest'	
suggest'ed	
suggest'ing	
sugges'tion	
suggest'ive	
suici'dal	
su'icide	
su'ing	
suit	
suitabil'ity	
suit'able	
suite	
suit'ed	
suit'ing	
sulk'y	
sul'len	
sul'lenness	
sul'phate	
sul'phide	
sul'phur	
sulphu'ric	
sul'tan	
sul'try	
sum	
sum'marily	
sum'marize	
sum'mary	
summed	
sum'mer	
sum'mit	
sum'mon	
sum'moned	
sum'mons	
sump'tuous	
sump'tuously	

sun	
sun'bathe	
sun'beam	
sun'burn	
sun'burnt	
Sun'day	
sun'der	
sun'dry	
sung	
sunk	
sunk'en	
sun'light	
sun'lit	
sun'rise	
sun'set	
sun'shine	
sun'spot	
sup	
su'per	
su'perable	
superabun'-dance	
superabun'-dant	
superan'nuate	
superan'nua-ted	
superannua'-tion	
superb'	
supercil'ious	
superfi'cial	
su'perfine	
superflu'ity	
super'fluous	
superhu'man	
superintend'	
superintend'ed	
superintend'-ence	
superintend'-ent	
supe'rior	
superior'ity	
super'lative	
super'latively	
su'permarine	
su'permarket	

supernat′ural	surf
supersede′	sur′face
superse′ded	surf′-board
superse′ding	sur′feit
superson′ic	sur′feited
supersti′tion	surge
supersti′tious	surged
supervise′	sur′geon
supervised′	sur′gery
supervi′sion	sur′gical
supervi′sor	sur′ly
sup′per	surmise′
supplant′	surmised′
supplant′ed	surmount′
supplant′ing	surmount′able
sup′ple	surmount′ed
sup′plement	surmount′ing
supplemen′tal	sur′name
supplemen′-tary	surpass′
sup′pliant	surpassed′
sup′plicant	sur′plus
sup′plicate	*surprise′*
supplica′tion	*surprised′*
supplied′	*surpri′sing*
supply′	surre′alism
support′	surren′der
support′able	surren′dered
support′ed	surrepti′tious
support′er	surround′
support′ing	surround′ed
suppose′	surround′ing
supposed′	⎰sur′tax, *n.*
suppo′sing	⎱surtax′, *v.*
supposi′tion	⎰sur′vey, *n.*
suppress′	⎱survey′, *v.*
suppressed′	surveyed′
suppress′ing	survey′ing
suppres′sion	survey′or
suprem′acy	survi′val
supreme′	survive′
supreme′ly	survived′
⎰sur′charge, *n.*	survi′ving
⎱surcharge′, *v.*	survi′vor
sure	susceptibil′ity
sure′ly	suscep′tible
sur′est	sus′pect, *n.*
sure′ty	

suspect', v.		swelled	
suspect'ed		swell'ing	
suspend'		swel'ter	
suspend'ed		swel'tered	
suspend'ing		swept	
suspense'		swerve	
suspen'sion		swerved	
suspi'cion		swerv'ing	
suspi'cious	or	swift	
		swift'er	
		swift'est	
suspi'ciously	or	swift'ly	
sustain'		swim	
sustained'		swim'mer	
sustain'ing		swim'ming	
sus'tenance		swim'mingly	
swag'ger		swin'dle	
swal'low		swin'dled	
swal'lowed		swin'dler	
swal'lowing		swin'dling	
swam		swine	
swamp		swing	
swamped		swing'ing	
swamp'y		Swiss	
swan		switch	
swap		switch'board	
swarm		switched	
swarmed		switch'ing	
swarm'ing		swiv'el	
swarth'y		swoll'en	
swathe		swoon	
sway		swoop	
swayed		sword	
sway'ing		swore	
swear		sworn	
sweat		swung	
sweat'er		syc'amore	
Swede		syllab'ic	
Swe'dish		syl'lable	
sweep		syl'labus	
sweep'er		syl'van	
sweep'ing		sym'bol	
sweet		symbol'ic	
sweet'er		sym'bolize	
sweet'est		symmet'rical	
sweet'ly		symmet'rically	
sweet'ness		sym'metry	
swell		*sympathet'ic*	

sympathet'-
  ically
sym'pathize
sym'pathized
sym'pathy
sym'phony
sympo'sium
symp'tom
syn'agogue
synchroniza'-
  tion
syn'chronize
syn'chronized
syn'chronizing

syn'dicate
syn'onym
synon'ymous
synop'sis
syn'thesis
synthet'ic
synthet'ically
syn'thetize
syr'inge
syr'up
sys'tem
systemat'ic
systemat'ical
systemat'ically

T

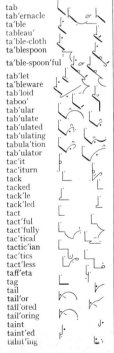

tab	take
tab'ernacle	ta'ken
ta'ble	take'-over
tableau'	ta'king
ta'ble-cloth	talc
ta'blespoon	tale
	tal'ent
ta'ble-spoon'ful	tal'ented
	tal'isman
tab'let	talk
ta'bleware	talk'ative
tab'loid	talk'er
taboo'	talk'ing
tab'ular	tall
tab'ulate	tall'er
tab'ulated	tallest
tab'ulating	tal'lied
tabula'tion	tal'low
tab'ulator	tal'ly
tac'it	tame
tac'iturn	tamed
tack	ta'mer
tacked	tam'per
tack'le	tam'pered
tack'led	tam'pering
tact	tan
tact'ful	tan'dem
tact'fully	tan'gent
tac'tical	tan'gible
tactic'ian	tan'gle
tac'tics	tang'o
tact'less	tank
taff'eta	tank'ard
tag	tan'ker
tail	tan'ner
tail'or	tan'nery
tail'ored	tan'nic
tail'oring	tan'nin
taint	tan'talize
taint'ed	tan'talizing
taint'ing	

193

tan'tamount	taunt'ing
tan'trum	taut
tap	tav'ern
tape	taw'dry
ta'per	taw'ny
tape'-record'er	tax
ta'pering	tax'able
tap'estry	taxa'tion
tapio'ca	taxed
tapped	tax'-free
tap'ping	tax'i
tar	tax'icab
tar'dily	tax'payer
tar'diness	tea
tar'dy	teach
tare	teach'er
tar'get	teach'ing
tar'iff	tea'cup
tar'mac	teak
tar'nish	team
tar'nished	tea'pot
tarpau'lin	tear, *n.*
tar'ried	tear, *v.*
tar'ring	tear'ful
tar'ry, *adj.*	tear'ing
tar'ry, *v.*	tease
tart	tea'spoon
tar'tan	tea'spoonful
tar'tar	tech'nical
tartar'ic	technical'ity
task	tech'nically
tas'sel	technique'
taste	technol'ogist
ta'sted	technol'ogy
taste'ful	te'dious
taste'fully	te'diously
taste'less	te'dium
taste'lessness	tee
ta'sting	teem
ta'sty	teemed
tat'ter	teem'ing
tat'tered	teen'age
tat'tle	teen'ager
tattoo'	teeth
tattooed'	teethe
taught	teeto'tal
taunt	teeto'taler,
taunt'ed	teeto'taller

tel'ecast		tempt'ing	
telegen'ic		ten	
tel'egram		ten'able	
tel'egraph		tena'cious	
telegraph'ic		tena'ciously	
teleg'raphist		tenac'ity	
teleg'raphy		ten'ancy	
telep'athy		ten'ant	
tel'ephone		tend	
telephon'ic		tend'ed	
teleph'onist		ten'dency	
teleph'ony		ten'der	
tele'photo		ten'dered	
tel'eprinter		ten'dering	
telepromp'ter		ten'derly	
tel'escope		tend'ing	
telescop'ic		ten'don	
tele'type		ten'ement	
tel'eview		ten'et	
tele'vise		ten'fold	
tel'evision		ten'nis	
tell		ten'or	
*tell'*er		tense	
*tell'*ing		tense'ly	
tell'-tale		ten'sion	
temer'ity		tent	
tem'per		ten'tacle	
tem'perament		ten'tative	
temperamen'tal		ten'tatively	
temperamen'tally		tenth	
tem'perance		ten'ure	
tem'perate		tep'id	
tem'perately		term	
tem'perature		termed	
tem'pered		ter'minable	
tem'pering		ter'minal	
tem'pest		ter'minate, *a.*	
tempes'tuous		ter'minate, *v.*	
tem'ple		ter'minated	
tem'poral		termina'tion	
tem'porarily		ter'minus	
tem'porary		ter'race	
tempt		ter'ra-cot'ta	
tempta'tion		terrain'	
tempt'ed		ter'rible	
		ter'ribly	
		ter'rier	
		terrif'ic	

ter'rified	theft
ter'rify	*their*
territo'rial	*theirs*
ter'ritory	*them*
ter'ror	theme
ter'rorism	*themselves'*
ter'rorize	then
terse	thence
terse'ly	thenceforth'
terylene'	*thencefor'ward*
test	(theolog'ical
tes'tament	(theolog'-
testamen'tary	ically
testa'tor	theol'ogist
testa'trix	theol'ogy
test'ed	the'orem
test'er	theoret'ical
tes'tified	theoret'ically
tes'tify	the'orist
testimo'nial	the'orize
tes'timony	the'ory
test'ing	*there*
tes'ty	*there'about*
teth'er	*thereaf'ter*
teth'ered	*thereat'*
text	*thereby'*
text'book	*there'for*
tex'tile	*there'fore*
tex'ture	*therefrom'*
than	*therein'*
(thank	*thereof'*
(thanked	*thereon'*
(thank'ful	*thereout'*
(thank'fully	*thereto'*
thank'fulness	*thereupon'*
thank'ing	*therewith'*
thank'less	therm
thanks	thermion'ic
thanks'giving	thermom'eter
that	ther'mos
thatch	ther'mostat
thatched	these
thaw	the'sis
thawed	they
the	thick
the'atre,	thick'en
the'ater	thick'ened
theat'rical	thick'ening

thick'er
thick'et
thick'ly
thick'ness
thief
thieves
thigh
thim'ble
thin
thine
thing
think
think'er
think'ing
thin'ly
thinned
thin'ner
third
third'ly
third'-rate'
thirds
thirst
thirst'ed
thirst'ing
thirst'y
thirteen'
thirteenth'
thir'tieth
thir'ty
this
this'tle
thorn
thorn'y
thor'ough
thor'oughbred
thor'oughfare
thor'oughly
thor'oughness
those
thou
though
thought
thought'ful
thought'fully
thought'ful-
ness
thought'less
thought'lessly

thought'less-
ness
thou'sand
thou'sandfold
thrash
thrashed
thrash'ing
thread
thread'bare
thread'ed
thread'ing
threat
threat'en
threat'ened
three
three-
quarters
thresh
thresh'old
threw
thrice
thrift
thrift'y
thrill
thrilled
thrill'er
thrill'ing
thrive
thri'ving
throat
throb
throbbed
throb'bing
throne
throng
thronged
throng'ing
throt'tle
through
throughout'
throw
throw'back
throw'ing
thrown
thrust
thrust'ing
thud
thumb

thump		tint	
thumped		tint'ed	
thun'der		tint'ing	
thun'dered		ti'ny	
Thurs'day		tip	
thus		tip'off	
thwart		tipped	
thwart'ed		tip'ping	
tick'et		tirade'	
tick'le		tire	
ti'dal		tired	
tide		tire'less	
ti'ded		tire'some	
ti'dings		tir'o	
ti'dy		tis'sue	
tie		Titan'ic	
tied		tit'-bit	
tier		tithe	
ti'ger		ti'tle	
tight		tit'ter	
tight'en		tit'ular	
tight'ened		*to*	
tight'ening		toast	
tight'ly		toast'ed	
tight'ness		toast'ing	
tile		tobac'co	
tiled		tobac'conist	
till, *n. and v.*		tobog'gan	
till, prep.		*today'*	
tilt		toe	
tilt'ed		tof'fee,	
tilt'ing		tof'fy	
tim'ber		*togeth'er*	
time		toil	
time'keeper		toiled	
time'table		toi'let	
tim'id		tok'en	
timid'ity		*told*	
tim'idly		tol'erable	
tim'orous		tol'erably	
tin		tol'erance	
tinc'ture		tol'erant	
tinge		tol'erate	
tin'gle		tol'erated	
tin'kle		tol'erating	
tinned		tolera'tion	
tin'plate		toll	
tin'sel		tolled	

toma'to		tot'ter	
tomb		touch	
tomb'stone		touched	
tomor'row		touch'ing	
ton		tough	
tone		tough'en	
tongs		tough'er	
tongue		tough'est	
ton'ic		tough'ness	
tonight'		tour	
ton'nage		tour'ing	
too		tour'ism	
took		tour'ist	
tool		tour'nament	
tooth		tour'ney	
tooth'ache		tout	
top		tout'ed	
to'paz		tout'ing	
top'-heavy		tow	
top'ic		*to'ward*	
top'ical		*to'wards*	
top'ple		towed	
top'pled		tow'el	
top'pling		tow'er	
torch		tow'ered	
tore		tow'ering	
tor'ment, *n.*		tow'ing	
torment', *v.*		town	
torment'ed		town'-clerk'	
torment'ing		town'ship	
torn		towns'man	
torna'do		toy	
torpe'do		toyed	
tor'pid		trace	
tor'rent		trace'able	
torren'tial		traced	
tor'rid		tra'cer	
tor'toise		tra'cing	
tor'tuous		track	
tor'ture		tracked	
tor'tured		track'less	
tor'turing		tract	
toss		tract'able	
tossed		trac'tion	
toss'ing		trac'tor	
to'tal		*trade*	
to'tally		tra'ded	
tote			

trade'-mark	(trans'fer, *n.*
tra'der	(transfer', *v.*
*trades'*man	trans'ferable
trades-u'nion	trans'ference
trades-u'nion-	transferred'
ism	transfix'
trade-u'nion	transform'
tra'ding	transforma'-
tradi'tion	tion
tradi'tional	transform'er
tradi'tionally	
traf'fic	transgress'
trag'edy	transgressed'
trag'ic	transgress'ing
trag'ically	transgres'sion
trail	tranship'
trail'er	tranship'ment
trail'ing	tran'sient
train	transist'or
trainee'	trans'it
train'er	transi'tion
train'ing	transi'tional
trait	trans'itory
trai'tor	translate'
tram	transla'ted
tramp	transla'ting
tramped	transla'tion
tramp'ing	transla'tor
tram'ple	transmis'sion
tram'pled	transmit'
tram'pling	transmit'ted
trance	transmit'ter
tran'quil	transmit'ting
tranquil'lity	transpa'rent
transact'	transpire'
transact'ed	transpired'
transact'ing	transpi'ring
transac'tion	transplant'
transatlan'tic	(trans'port, *n.*
	(transport', *v.*
transcend'	transporta'-
transcend'ed	tion
transcend'ent	transport'ed
	transpose'
transcribe'	transship'
	transship'ment
tran'script	trap
transcrip'tion	

trap'-door'	tri'bal
trapeze'	tribe
trapped	tribula'tion
trap'ping	tribu'nal
trash	
trav'el	trib'une
trav'elled,	trib'utary
trav'eled	trib'ute
trav'eller,	trick
trav'eler	tricked
trav'elogue	trick'ery
trav'erse	trick'le
trav'ersed	trick'led
treach'erous	trick'y
treach'ery	*tried*
treac'le	trien'nial
tread	tri'fle
tread'ing	tri'fled
trea'son	tri'fling
treas'ure	trig'ger
treas'urer	trim
treas'ury	trim'ly
treat	trimmed
treat'ed	trin'ity
treat'ing	trin'ket
trea'tise	tri'o
treat'ment	trip
trea'ty	tripe
treb'le	trip'le
tree	trip'lex
trel'lis	trip'licate, *n.,*
trem'ble	*a.*
trem'bled	trip'licate, *v.*
trem'bling	trite
tremen'dous	trite'ly
trem'or	trite'ness
trem'ulous	tri'umph
trench	trium'phal
trench'ant	trium'phant
trend	trium'phantly
tres'pass	tri'umphed
tres'passed	triv'ial
tres'passer	trivial'ity
tres'passing	trod
tress	trodd'en
tri'al	trol'ley
tri'angle	troop
trian'gular	troop'er

tro'phy		try	
trop'ical		try'ing	
trot		try'-on	
trot'ted		tryst	
trot'ting		tub	
troub'le		tube	
troub'led		tuber'cular	
troub'lesome		tuberculo'sis	
troub'ling		tuber'culous	
troub'lous		tu'bing	
trough		tu'bular	
trou'sers		tuck	
trousseau'		Tu'dor	
trout		Tues'day	
trow'el		tuft	
tru'ant		tug	
truce		tui'tion	
truck		tu'lip	
tru'culence		tum'ble	
tru'culent		tum'bled	
trudge		tum'bler	
trudged		tu'mult	
trudg'ing		tumul'tuous	
true		tune	
tru'est		tuned	
tru'ism		tuneful	
trump		tune'fully	
trump'et		tu'ner	
trump'eter		tu'nic	
trun'dle		tu'ning	
trunk		tun'nel	
trunk'-call		tur'bine	
truss		tur'bulent	
trust		turf	
trust'ed		Turk	
trustee'		tur'key	
trust'ful		tur'moil	
trust'fully		turn	
trust'ing		turned	
trust'ingly		turn'er	
trust'worthi- ness		turn'ing	
		turn'ing-point	
trust'worthy		tur'nip	
trust'y		turn'over	
truth		turn'stile	
truth'ful		turn'table	
truth'fulness		tur'pentine	
truths		tur'ret	

tur'tle	
tusk	
tus'sle	
tu'tor	
tuto'rial	
tu'tors	
twad'dle	
tweed	
twee'zers	
twelfth	
twelve	
twen'tieth	
twen'ty	
twice	
twig	
twi'light	
twill	
twin	
twine	
twinge	
twi'ning	
twin'kle	
twin'kled	
twin'kling	
twist	
twist'ed	
twist'ing	
twitch	
two	
two'fold	

two-seater	
two-some	
ty'ing	
type	
type'script	
type'writer	
type'writing	
type'written	
ty'phoid	
typhoon'	
typ'ical	
typ'ified	
typ'ify	
ty'pist	
typograph'ic	
typograph'ical	
typog'raphy	
typol'ogy	
tyran'nic	
tyran'nical	
tyran'nically	
tyr'annize	
tyr'annized	
tyr'annous	
tyr'anny	
ty'rant	
tyre	
ty'ro	

U

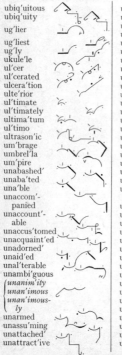

ubiq'uitous
ubiq'uity

ug'lier

ug'liest
ug'ly
ukule'le
ul'cer
ul'cerated
ulcera'tion
ulte'rior
ul'timate
ul'timately
ultima'tum
ul'timo
ultrason'ic
um'brage
umbrel'la
um'pire
unabashed'
unaba'ted
una'ble
unaccom'-
  panied
unaccount'-
  able
unaccus'tomed
unacquaint'ed
unadorned'
unaid'ed
unal'terable
unambi'guous
{ unanim'ity
{ unan'imous
{ unan'imous-
  ly
unarmed
unassu'ming
unattached'
unattract'ive

unau'thorized
unavail'able
unavoid'able
unaware'
unbal'anced
unbear'able
unbecom'ing
unbelief'
un*believ*'able
unbeliev'er
unbeliev'ing
unbend'
unbi'assed
unblem'ished
unborn'
unbound'ed
unbrok'en
un*called*'
uncan'ny
unceas'ing
unceas'ingly
unceremo'-
  nious
uncer'tain
unchal'lenged
unchanged'
unchar'itable
unciv'il
unciv'ilized
un'cle
unclean'
uncom'fortable
uncom'mon
uncom'monly
unconcern'
unconcern'edly
uncondi'tional
unconge'nial
unconnect'ed
uncon'scious

204

unconstitu'-
tional

unconstitu'-
tionally

uncontrol'lable

uncontrolled'

unconven'tional

uncouth'

uncov'er

uncul'tivated

uncut'

unda'ted

undaunt'ed

undeci'ded

undefend'ed

undefiled'

undefined'

undeliv'ered

undeni'able

un'der

un'dercarriage

und'ercoat

un'dercurrent

un'derdog

under-es'ti-
mate, n.

under-es'ti-
mate, v.

under-es'ti-
mated

undergo'

undergrad'uate

un'derground

un'dergrowth

un'derhand

un'derline

underly'ing

underneath'

un'der-nourished

un'derpass

un'der-pri'-
vileged

underrate'

under-sec're-
tary

un'derstaffed

understand'

understate'ment

understood'

un'derstudy

undertake'

un'dertone

un'derwear

un'derworld

un'derwriter

undeserved'

undesir'able

undeterred'

undisclosed'

undisturbed'

undivi'ded

undo'

undoubt'ed

undoubt'edly

undress'

undue'

un'dulating

undu'ly

unearned'

uneas'ily

uneas'y

uneconom'ic

unemploy'able

unemployed'

unemploy'-
ment

une'qual

une'qualled

une'qually

uner'ring

uner'ringly

une'ven

une'venly

uneventful

unexam'pled

unexpect'ed

unexpect'edly

unfailing

unfair'

unfaith'ful

unfamil'iar

unfash'ionable

unfa'vourable

unfeel'ing

unfeigned'

unfert'ilized	u'nison
unfin'ished	u'nit
unfit'	unite'
unflag'ging	uni'ted
unflat'tering	u'nity
unfold'	*univer'sal*
unforeseen'	*universal'ity*
	univer'sally
unforgett'able	*u'niverse*
	univer'sity
unfor'tunate	unjust'
unfor'tunately	unjust'ifiable
	unjus'tified
unfound'ed	unkind'
unfriend'ly	unknown'
unfulfilled'	unlaw'ful
unfurl'	unless'
unfurled'	unlike'
unfur'nished	unlike'ly
ungen'tlemanly	unlim'ited
ungov'ernable	unload'
ungra'cious	unlock'
ungrate'ful	unluck'ily
unguard'ed	unluck'y
unhap'pily	unman'nerly
unhap'py	unmind'ful
unharmed'	unmista'kable
unhealth'y	unmit'igated
unhes'itatingly	unmoved'
unhook'	unnat'ural
unhurt'	unnec'essarily
unhygien'ic	unnec'essary
uni'fied	unno'ticed
[*u'niform*	unobtain'able
uniform'ity	unoffi'cial
u'niformly]	unor'ganized
u'nify	unorth'odox
unilat'eral	unpaid'
unimpaired'	unpal'atable
unim*por'tant*	unpar'alleled
unin*'fluenced*	unpleas'ant
unin*formed'*	unpleas'antly
unin*tel'ligible*	unpop'ular
uninten'tional	unprec'edented
uninterrupt'ed	unpre*j'udiced*
u'nion	unpremed'ita-
U'nionist	ted
unique'	unprepared'

un*prin'cipaled*	unspa'ringly
un*produc'tive*	unspe'cified
unprof'itable	unsta'ble
unprotect'ed	unstead'ily
unprovoked'	unstead'y
un*pub'lished*	unstud'ied
unqual'ified	unsuccess'ful
{ un*ques'tion-able*	unsuccess'fully
un*ques'tion-ably*	unsuit'able
	unsurpassed'
unrav'el	un*suspect'ed*
	un*suspect'ing*
unre'alizable	unswerv'ing
or	un*sympathet'ic*
unrea'sonable	untaxed'
unrelat'ed	unti'diness
unreli'able	unti'dy
unremu'nera-tive	untie'
	untied'
un*represent'ed*	until'
unreserv'edly	untime'ly
unrest'	untir'ing
unrestrict'ed	un'to
unru'ly	un*told'*
unsafe'	unto'ward
un*satisfac'tory*	un*tried'*
unscrew'	untrod'den
unscrewed'	untrue'
unscru'pulous	untruth'
unseen'	{ un*u'sual*
un*self'ish*	un*u'sually*
un*self'ishly*	unva'rying
un*self'ishness*	unveil'
unset'tle	unveiled'
unset'tled	unwar'rantable
unsight'ed	unwar'ranted
unsight'ly	unwea'ried
unskil'ful	unwel'come
unskilled'	unwell'
unso'ciable	unwhole'some
unsoiled'	unwield'y
unsold'	unwil'ling
uncolic'ited	unwil'lingly
unsophis'tica-ted	unwise'
	unwise'ly
unsound'	unwit'tingly
unsound'ly	unwork'able
unspa'ring	unwor'thy

unwrit'ten	u'sable
unyield'ing	u'sage
up	use
up'bringing	used
upheav'al	use'ful
upheave'	use'fully
upheld'	use'fulness
uphill'	use'less
uphold'	use'lessly
uphold'ing	use'lessness
uphol'ster	u'ser
uphol'sterer	ush'er
uphol'stery	ush'ered
uplift'	usherette'
upon'	u'sing
up'per	u'sual,
up'permost	u'sually
up'right'	u'surer
up'roar	usurp'
uproar'ious	u'sury
uproot'	uten'sil
upset'	util'ity
up'surge	utiliza'tion
up'swing	u'tilize
up'wards	u'tilized
ur'ban	u'tilizing
urbane'	ut'most
urban'ity	Uto'pia
ur'chin	ut'ter
urge	ut'terance
ur'gency	ut'tered
ur'gent	ut'tering
ur'gently	ut'terly
urn	ut'termost
us	

V

va'cancy	val'ued
va'cant	valve
vacate'	valv'ular
vaca'ted	vamp
vaca'ting	vam'pire
vaca'tion	van
vac'cinate	vanil'la
vac'cinated	van'ish
vaccina'tion	van'ished
vac'cine	van'ishing
vac'illate	van'ity
vac'illated	van'quish
vac'illating	van'tage
vacilla'tion	vap'id
vac'uous	vap'orizer
vac'uum	va'pour,
vag'abond	va'por
vaga'ry	va'riable
va'grancy	va'riance
va'grant	va'riant
vague	varia'tion
vague'ly	va'ried
vain	vari'ety
vain'ly	va'rious
vale	var'nish
valedic'tory	var'nishing
val'ency	va'ry
val'et	va'rying
val'iant	vase
val'iantly	Vas'eline
val'id	vas'sal
valid'ity	vast
valise'	vast'ly
val'ley	vat
val'orous	Vat'ican
val'our	vaude'ville
val'uable	vault
valua'tion	vault'ed
val'ue	vault'ing
	vaunt

209

vaunt'ed	ven'ue	vera'cious
veal	verac'ity	
veer	veran'dah	
veered	verb	
veer'ing	ver'bal	
veg'etable	verba'tim	
vegeta'rian *or*	ver'biage	
	verbose'	
vegeta'rianism *or*	verbos'ity	
vegeta'tion	ver'dant	
ve'hemence	ver'dict	
ve'hement	ver'dure	
ve'hemently	verge	
ve'hicle	verifica'tion	
vehic'ular	ver'ified	
veil	ver'ify	
veiled	ver'ily	
vein	ver'itable	
vel'lum	vermil'ion	
veloc'ity	ver'min	
velour'	ver'satile	
vel'vet	versatil'ity	
velveteen'	verse	
vend'er,	ver'sion	
vend'or	ver'sus	
vendet'ta	ver'tebrae	
vend'or	ver'tical	
(*legal term*)	*ver'y*	
veneer'	ves'sel	
ven'erable	vest	
ven'erate	vest'ed	
venera'tion	ves'tibule	
Vene'tian	ves'tige	
ven'geance	vest'ment	
ve'nial	ves'try	
ven'ison	ves'ture	
ven'om	vet'eran	
ven'omous	vet'erinary	
vent	ve'to	
ven'tilate	vex	
ven'tilated	vexa'tion	
ventila'tion	vexa'tious	
ven'tilator	vexed	
ven'ture	vi'a	
ven'tured	vi'aduct	
ven'turesome	vi'al	
ven'turing	vi'brant	

vi'brate	viola'tion
vi'brated	vi'olence
vibra'tion	vi'olent
vic'ar	vi'olently
vica'rious	vi'olet
vice	violin'
vice-*chair*'man	violin'ist
vice-pres'ident	vi'per
vice-*prin*'ci*pal*	vir'gin
vice'roy	vir'ile
vic'e ver'sa	viril'ity
vicin'ity	vir'tual
vic'ious	vir'tue
vic'iously	virtuos'ity
vicis'situde	vir'tuous
vic'tim	vir'ulence
victimiza'tion	vir'ulent
vic'tor	vi'sa
victo'rious	vis'age
vic'tory	vis'cous
vict'uals	vi'sé
vid'eo	visibil'ity
vie	vis'ible
view	vi'sion
viewed	vi'sionary
vig'il	vis'it
vig'ilance	visita'tion
vig'ilant	vis'ited
vig'orous	vis'iting
vig'our	vis'itor
vile	vis'ta
vil'la	vis'ual
vil'lage	visualiza'tion
vil'lain	vis'ualize
vil'lainous	vi'tal
vil'lainy	vital'ity
vim	vi'tally
vin'dicate	vi'tamin
vin'dicated	vi'tiate
vindica'tion	vi'tiated
vindic'tive	vitriol'ic
vindic'tively	vitu'perate
vine	vitupera'tion
vin'egar	viva'cious
vine'yard	vivac'ity
vin'tage	viv'id
vi'olate	viv'idly
vi'olated	vivisec'tion

vocab′ulary	volunteer′
vo′cal	volunteered′
vo′calist	volunteer′ing
vocaliza′tion	vora′cious
voca′tion	vo′tary
voca′tional	vote
vocif′erous	vo′ted
vod′ka	vo′ter
vogue	vouch
voice	vouch′er
void	vouchsafe
vol′atile	vow
vol′-au-vent′	vowed
volcan′ic	vow′el
volca′no	voy′age
vol′ley	vul′canite
volt	vul′canize
volt′age	vul′gar
volubil′ity	vulgar′ity
vol′uble	vul′garly
vol′ume	vulnerabil′ity
volu′minous	vul′nerable
	vul′ture
vol′untarily	vy′ing
vol′untary	

W

wad	walk'-over
wad'ding	wall
wade	wal'let
wa'ded	wal'low
wa'ding	wall'paper
wa'fer	wal'nut
waf'fle	wal'rus
waft	waltz
waft'ed	waltzed
wag	wan
wage	wand
wage'-freeze	wan'der
wa'ger	wan'dered
wag'on,	wan'derer
wag'gon	wan'dering
waif	wane
wail	want
wailed	want'ed
wain'scot	wan'ton
wain'scotting	war
waist	war'ble
waist'coat	ward
wait	ward'en
wait'ed	ward'er
wait'er	ward'robe
wait'ing-list	ware'house
wait'ing-room	wares
wait'ress	war'fare
waive	war'ily
wake	war'like
wake'ful	warm
wake'fulness	warmed
wa'ken	warm'er
wa'kening	warm'est
walk	warm'-hearted
walked	warmth
walk'er	warn
walk'ing	warned
walk'ing-stick	warn'ing
walk'-out	War'-Office

213

warp	way'faring
war'rant	way'side
war'ranted	*we*
war'ranty	weak
war'rior	weak'en
war'ship	weak'er
wa'ry	weak'ness
was	weal
wash	wealth
wash'able	wealth'ier
washed	wealth'iest
wash'er	wealth'y
wash'ing	weap'on
wash'out	wear
wasp	wear'able
waste	wear'er
wast'ed	wear'ied
waste'ful	wear'ing
waste'fully	wear'isome
wa'sting	wear'y
watch	wear'ying
watched	weath'er
watch'er	weath'erproof
watch'ful	weave
watch'fulness	weav'er
watch'ing	weav'ing
watch'man	web
wa'ter	wed'ding
wa'terfall	wedge
wa'terfront	wedged
	wedg'ing
wa'termark	Wednes'day
wa'termelon	weed
wa'terproof	week
wa'tershed	week'day
wa'tertight	week-end'
watt	week'ly
wave	weep
waved	weigh
wave'length	weighed
wa'ver	weigh'ing
wa'vered	weight
wa'vering	weight'y
wa'ving	weir
wa'vy	weird
wax	wel'come
way	wel'comed
way'farer	wel'coming

weld		which		
weld'ed		whichev'er		
weld'ing		whiff		
wel'fare		while		
well		whiled		
well-known'		whilst		
well-mean'ing		whim		
Welsh		whim'per		
wel'ter		whim'pered		
went		whim'pering		
wept		whim'sical		
were		whine		
west		whined		
west'erly		whi'ning		
west'ern		whip		
west'ward		whirl		
wet		whirled		
whale		whirl'ing		
wharf		whirl'pool		
wharf'age		whirl'wind		
what		whis'key,		
whatev'er		whis'ky		
*whats*oev'er		whis'per		
wheat		whis'pered		
wheel		whis'pering		
wheel'-base		whist		
wheeled		whis'tle		
when		whis'tled		
whence		whit		
whenev'er		white		
whensoev'er		whith'er		
where		*whithersoev'er*		
where'abouts		whit'tle		
whereas'		whiz		
whereat'		*who*		
whereby'		*whoev'er*		
		whole		
where'fore		whole'heart'ed		
		whole-		
where'*in*		heart'edly		
whereinsoev'er		whole'sale		
whereof'		whole'some		
whereon'		whol'ly		
wheresoev'er		whom		
whereto'		whoop		
whereupon'		*whose*		
wherev'er		*whosoev'er*		
wherewithal'		why		
wheth'er				

wick		wine'-glass	
wick'ed		wing	
wick'er		wink	
wick'et		win'ner	
wide		win'ning	
wide'ly		win'some	
wi'den		win'ter	
wi'dened		win'terly	
wi'dening		win'try	
wi'der		wipe	
wide'spread		wiped	
wid'ow		wi'ping	
wid'ower		wire	
width		wired	
wield		wire'less	
wife		wir'y	
wig		wis'dom	
wild		wise	
wild'er		wise'ly	
wil'derness		wi'ser	
wild'est		wi'sest	
wild'ly		*wish*	
wil'ful		*wished*	
wil'fully		*wish'ing*	
wil'fulness		wist'ful	
will		wist'fully	
willed		wit	
will'ing		*with*	
wil'lingly		withal'	
wil'low		withdraw'	
wilt		withdraw'al	
wi'ly		withdrawn'	
win		withdrew'	
wince		with'er	
winced		with'ered	
wind, *n.*		withheld'	
wind, *v.*		withhold'	
wind'fall		*within'*	
wind'ing		*without'*	
win'dow		withstand'	
win'dow-dressing		withstood'	
wind'screen		wit'ness	
wind'-tunnel		wit'ticism	
wind'ward		wit'ty	
wine		wiz'ard	
wine'-cellar		wob'ble	
		wob'bled	
		wob'bling	

woke			wor'sen		
wolf			wor'ship		
wom'an			worst		
wom'anhood			worst'ed		
wom'anly			worth		
wom'en			wor'thier		
won			wor'thiest		
won'der			wor'thily		
won'dered			worth'less		
{won'derful			worth'lessness		
{won'derfully			worthwhile'		
won'dering			wor'thy		
won'deringly			*would*		
won'drous			*would-be*		
won'drously			wound, *n., v.*		
won't			wound, *v.*		
wont			wound'ing		
wont'ed			wove		
wood			wo'ven		
wood'en			wran'gle		
wood'work			wrap		
wool			wrapped		
wool'len			wrap'per		
wooll'ies			wrap'ping		
wool'sack			wrath		
word			wrath'ful		
word'ed			wreath		
word'ing			wreathe		
word'y			wreck		
wore			wreck'age		
work			wrecked		
work'able			wreck'ing		
worked			wrench		
work'er			wrenched		
work'ing			wrench'ing		
work'less			wrest		
work'man			wres'tle		
work'manship			wres'tled		
work'shop			wrest'ling		
world			wretch		
world'ly			wretch'ed		
world'wide			wretch'edness		
worm			wrig'gle		
worn			wright		
wor'ried			wring		
wor'ry			wring'er		
wor'rying			wrin'kle		
worse			wrist		

wrist'let		
wrist'watch		
writ		
write		
wri'ter		
write'-up		
writhe		
writhed		
wri'ting		
writ'ten		
wrong		

wronged	
wrong'ful	
wrong'fully	
wrong'ly	
wrote	
wroth	
wrought'	
wrought'-iron'	
wrung	
wry	

X

xan'thium
xantho-
  car'pous
xe'nial
xenog'amy
xenoglos'(s)ia
xen'on
xenophob'ia
xera'sia
xero'graphy
xeroph'agy
xerophthal'mia

xero'sis

xiph'oid
X-ray'
X-rays
xy'lem
xy'locarp
xy'lograph
xy'loid
xyloi'din(e)
xylom'eter
xy'lonite
xyloph'agous
xy'lophone
xys'ter
xys'tus

Y

yacht
yacht'ing
yank
yard
yarn
yawn
yawned
yawn'ing
ye
yea
year
year'book
year'ly
yearn
yearned
yearn'ing
yeast
yell
yel'low
yelp
yelped
yelp'ing
yes
yes'terday

yet
yew
Yid'dish
yield
yield'ed
yo'ghourt
yoke
yo'kel
yolk
yon'der
you
young
young'er
young'est
young'ster
your
yourself'
yourselves'
youth
youth'ful
youth'fulness
Yule
Yule'tide

Z

za'ny
zap'tieh
zare'ba

zar'nich
zax
ze'a
zeal
zeal'ot
zeal'ous
zeal'ously
ze'bra
zed
zed'oary
zeit'geist
zen
zen'ith
zeph'yr
ze'ro
zest
zest'ful
zig'zag
zinc
zin'nia
zip
zip'-fas'tener

zir'con
zith'er
zo'diac
zo'nal
zone
zo'ning
zoolog'ical
zool'ogist
zool'ogy
zoom
Zu'lu
zy'gal
zygodac'tyl
zygo'ma
zygomat'ic
zyg'ote
zyme
zymol'ogist
zymol'ogy
zymom'eter
zy'moscope
zymo'sis
zymot'ic
zy'murgy
zy'thum